A COMFORT OF
CATS

DOREEN TOVEY

summersdale

Sadly, Doreen Tovey died in 2008, aged nearly ninety. She had thousands of fans of all nationalities and was surrounded by good friends and of course her two cats, Rama and Tiah, who were with her almost to the end. Over fifty years since her first book was published, she has delighted generations of owners of Siamese cats.

Also by Doreen Tovey

A COMFORT OF CATS

First published by Michael Joseph Ltd in 1980

This edition published in 2008 by Summersdale Publishers Ltd.

Copyright © Doreen Tovey 1980.

All rights reserved.

The right of Doreen Tovey to be identified as the author of this work has been asserted in accordance with sections 77 and 78 of the Copyright, Designs and Patents Act 1988.

Summersdale Publishers Ltd
46 West Street
Chichester
West Sussex
PO19 1RP
UK

www.summersdale.com

Printed and bound in Great Britain

ISBN 13: 978-1-84024-655-1

Praise for *Cats in the Belfry*

'The most enchanting cat book ever'

Jilly Cooper

'If you read *Cats in the Belfry* the first time round, be prepared to be enchanted all over again. If you haven't, then expect to laugh out loud, shed a few tears and be totally captivated by Doreen's stories of her playful and often naughty Siamese cats'

***Your Cat* magazine**

'A funny and poignant reflection of life with a Siamese, that is full of cheer'

The Good Book Guide

Praise for *Cats in May*

'If you loved Doreen Tovey's *Cats in the Belfry* you won't want to miss the sequel, *Cats in May*... This witty and stylish tale will have animal lovers giggling to the very last page'

***Your Cat* magazine**

Praise for *The New Boy*

'Delightful stories of Tovey's irrepressible Siamese cats'

Publishing News

One

There was a time when the sitting-room of our small West Country cottage would have done credit to a Christmas card with its white walls, dark-beamed ceiling, wine-coloured carpet, chairs covered in pale green rose-patterned linen and here and there a cherished piece of family china or glass – but that was before we had Siamese cats.

The Copeland cabbage-leaf bowl belonging to Charles's grandmother which stood in one of the wide-silled windows, for instance... that departed from the family inheritance when our first Siamese, Sugieh, had kittens and some friends whom we invited to see them brought their own Siamese, James, along as well.

Until then Sugieh and James had been the best of friends. She'd stayed with him as a kitten herself, while we were on holiday, and with the air of an indulgent elder brother

7

he'd taught her to dig holes in the garden (she'd previously thought you went indoors to your earthbox for that); how to climb trees (within no time she was zooming up and down like a particularly ebullient piece of thistledown while he was hopelessly stuck); how to add a touch of Siamese variety to the everyday things of life... To quote one example the pair of them chose, entirely of their own accord, to sleep together in the cabinet of a record-player whose works had gone for repair. It was in the dining-room and according to James's owners the effect when people came to supper and two Siamese heads suddenly appeared through the hole where the turntable should have been – one big, dark and gravely contemplative, the other small, blue and spectacularly cross-eyed – was quite demoralising. More than one guest missed aim with his soup spoon as a result.

They thought Sugieh would be pleased to see James when they brought him over to our place, and when she met him in the garden she was. It was only when they came indoors and Solomon, biggest and most bat-brained of her kittens, spat at him saying to Watch Out Everybody, he'd come to Kidnap Them, that the balloon went up. By the time it came down again Sugieh, in her role of devoted mother, had bitten James: somebody had bitten James's mistress... in the explosive battle-of-the-planets action that followed we were never quite sure who, though we rather believed it to be Sugieh as well since James appeared to be far too busy trying to escape up the curtains... and the Copeland bowl was in pieces on the floor.

That was the first of our treasures to hit the dust. A Bristol glass jug and the porcelain figure of a Breton

spinning-woman that stood on the bureau went next, during the course of the round-the-room steeplechases devised by Sugieh for the indoor exercise of her children. That she was behind the idea was obvious from the fact that whenever, hearing what sounded like the beginning of a cavalry charge, we came running to see what we could rescue, Sugieh would be standing on the corner of the Welsh dresser, head stuck out like a swimming instructor, inciting them in her raucous Siamese soprano to Go Faster, they'd never catch a mouse at That Speed, or to Jump the Table Lamp, never mind if they knocked it off, old Charles could Always Mend It.

He couldn't mend the jug. It was shattered beyond repair. He did mend the Breton spinning-woman, whose only damage was that her head had come off. The snag was, though, that she sat posed with her tall, top-heavy Breton headdress bent attentively over her spindle. The repair held all right in normal weather but when it rained or we got hill-mist, as we do so often in the West Country, the glue would soften (this was before the days of waterproof resins) and her head, being heavy, would fall off.

We got quite used to sticking it on again and really thought nothing of it. Came the day, however, when we acquired a household help. I was doing a full-time job at that time and having somebody to clean the place was wonderful. The floors shone, the brass gleamed, the tidiness was a joy to come home to. Unfortunately, after only a few weeks of lifting up our hearts, Mrs Pearson said she didn't like being on her own in the cottage. She was used to having somebody to talk to, she said, and when I asked whether she didn't find the cats company – Solomon in particular

talked a lot – she said that was part of the trouble. She'd be working away listening to the silence, there'd suddenly be this awful yell – and when her heart stopped racing enough for her to turn round, he'd be sitting in the doorway *looking* at her.

Solomon did tend to watch people. Knowing his concern for his stomach he was probably only making sure they weren't eating something behind his back but I appreciated that to an outsider the sight of a Siamese sitting bolt upright in a doorway that had been empty a moment before, looking like a feline Fu Manchu-cum-Judge Jeffreys, and Little Did They Know, said his expression, what he'd seen them Doing before they spotted him... I quite *appreciated* that it put one off a bit.

I explained that he liked watching people and his wail was only by way of conversation – he was probably enquiring what was for supper and did she have an odd biscuit on her. It was no use. The following week the Breton woman's head fell off while Mrs Pearson was on the other side of the room dusting the mantelpiece, and while she was standing there rooted to the spot thinking the spirits must have done it (it seemed she hadn't realised that the head was stuck on and I'd never thought to tell her) from the doorway, to add to the effect, came that straight-from-the-graveyard wail...

As usual she'd gone before we got home but that night she came back to see us. She knew we wouldn't believe her, she said. We'd think *she'd* broken the ornament. It wasn't because of that, though, that she was giving us her notice. When it came to our having ghosts as well as Siamese cats...

In vain we plied her with sherry and explained about the figure being broken already. Her nerves wouldn't

stand any more, she said. She was going to work at the mushroom farm.

She did too, joining the happy band of local ladies who were picked up by private bus on the green in the morning and wafted off to a village three miles away where, cutting mushrooms to music in long rows of steaming sheds, they could talk to one another all day, with no ghosts, Siamese cats or other people's muddles to dismay them and, feeling as liberated and avant-garde as their town sisters, bowled back in the afternoon several pounds better off with a bag of mushrooms for their husbands' teas. It thus being impossible to get a replacement for her – *everybody* worked at the mushroom farm – I went back to doing the housework myself and the state of the cottage slipped steadily downhill.

Solomon ripped a hole through the staircarpet. Working industriously away in the hall Sheba, his sister (we kept the two of them after Sugieh died), converted an entire hide armchair to suede. The pair of them swung like cuckoo-clock pendulums on the curtains and chased over the pale green covers in the sitting-room till they were more of an elephant grey...

I washed the covers, of course. I was eternally washing them, much to Solomon's approval. With every wash they shrank still further and as he was now banned from the hall (we'd had to replace the staircarpet and were trying to keep him away from it) he'd transferred his exercises to the chairs instead and the tighter the covers fitted, the better.

When he'd reduced them to the state where even Charles noticed they had holes in them we replaced them with heavy-quality stretch nylon. Easier to wash – but the cats'

claws didn't, as the salesman assured us they would, slide over them. They latched into them like fish-hooks and within weeks we had laddered stretch astrakhan. What did we do, therefore, when at fourteen and a half our dark man died of kidney trouble, leaving us with an ache in our hearts and the stuffing hanging out of the lounge suite? We decided to get another boy as much like Solomon as we could.

Siamese have that effect on people. Noisy, destructive, imperious to the point of autocracy – one look from those compelling blue eyes and they have you in bondage for life. I wouldn't put it past them to have decided to have eyes like that deliberately – to set them apart from other cats and stop people in their tracks. Add to the eyes the Oriental mask, those long thin legs, that tail like a taper, the voice like a rusty saw, the air of aristocracy... the knowledge that, despite such innate superiority, Solomon had loved us with all his heart, as dearly as we loved him...

To heck with the furniture. We went out and got Seeley. If *he* wrecked the staircarpet – there were more important things in life.

As a matter of fact he didn't. One thing we can vouch for after all our years of Siamese cat-keeping is that, though they are universally destructive, even the most basic of their Machiavellian traits varies according to the cat. All of them claw things like Welshmen playing harps, for instance, but while Solomon practised pizzicatos on the staircarpet, Seeley did his on the draught-proofing round the doors. Ours is an old cottage, draughts whizz in like Atlantic gales and the door-surrounds are, or rather were, fitted with foam-rubber stripping – which Seeley, any time he was shut

out of a room or just simply mad about something, ripped out with impassioned fervour and scattered in pieces over the floor.

Seeley was four when he went out one morning for his pre-breakfast look-round and was never seen again. I have told his story before. I shall never, ever, forget the months of fruitless, heartbreaking searching. Even now, more than three years later, wherever we go we look at every Siamese we see. We still cherish the hope that if – which is one of the possibilities that might have happened that nightmare Sunday morning – he climbed into a stationary car and was carried away by accident, one of these days we might still find our dear dark bumble-head again.

When he'd been missing for four months we could stand it no longer and got Saska, our present Seal Point boy. We had Shebalu, of course, the Blue Point girl who'd succeeded Sheba some two years previously, but for things to be right there had to be a set of gangling, spider-thin brown legs racing up the stairs, vanishing round corners or disappearing at top speed from the scene of any domestic crime as well as four slightly smaller blue ones – and anyway Shebalu missed Seeley as much as we did.

Revel she might in coming to bed with us for company, sleeping with her head on my shoulder, no longer being pushed aside by someone who took it for granted that he always had Number One Place – but she still never ate without glancing to see if he was eating beside her; never went out without stopping to scan the hillside or look expectantly up the garden for a cat who never came.

So we got Saska. He didn't waste time on the draught-proofing. From the beginning he was a kitten who worked

things out. His reasoning was simple. Clawing at doors would get you nowhere. Tunnelling under them was the obvious way. We now have carpets with rounded corners where he hooked them up in front of any door that thwarted him and, when he found he couldn't burrow underneath, chewed them vengefully, with his head turned sideways, as determinedly as a dog.

We also have vinyl protective pieces that fit over the corners of the carpets. A little late in the day, but they do prevent further erosion – except when anyone special is coming and we whip the vinyl pieces off. They look rather odd and people might think us eccentric so I expose the chewed-up corners, laughingly explain about Saska's idiosyncrasy, shut him and Shebalu out into the hall when it's time to eat so they can't climb over people's plates. And what do I see – what do I *know* I will see – when, the food cleared away, I open the door to allow them to rejoin the party? Two cats sitting bolt upright on the other side of it and, with the vinyl obligingly removed, a bite more chewed off the carpet. Sass the Indomitable has struck again.

The cottage, as I say, looks rather different nowadays. We have these odd-looking vinyl corner-pieces. Our sitting-room carpet is a mottled tan. Not so aesthetically pleasing as the red one but it doesn't show muddy paw-prints, or the spots where they splash their supper milk, or the places where – being great ones for Better Health for Cats – having eaten enough grass to sink a battleship, they come in and sick it up with gusto on the floor.

We have a settee and armchairs in hide-grained vinyl now. It looks like leather, people comment on its being saddle-backed – gives the room quite a ranch effect, they

say. Maybe it does, but this is an English cottage. I sigh for my pale green covers of former days. Vinyl can be wiped, however, and the cats never attempt to claw it – which sounds incredible, but is absolutely true. Some people say it's the smell of it, others the slippery texture – the fact remains that whereas they will strop on leather or fabric like tempestuous impresarios, for some peculiar reason vinyl is taboo.

I wish I could say the same about woodwork. Sass, for instance, can jump like a Mexican bean. When we take them over to the orchard he soars spectacularly over the bars which block the entrance – up, over and down from standing, to the astonishment of all who see him, while Shebalu clambers primly over them like one of the *Pirates of Penzance* girls over the rocks. Indoors, however, it is she who leaps without a second thought five feet up to the back window of the living-room – the high one that looks out on to the hillside where Annabel and her friends the magpies roam. And what does Sass the Indomitable do when, seeing her craning her neck at something that appears to be interesting, he decides to join her in the window sill? He clambers laboriously, as he did when a kitten, up the back of one of our antique carved chairs.

Then it was delightful, watching him heave his small white body up the pattern of acorns and dog-roses like a climber ascending the Matterhorn, invariably losing his nerve halfway up and bawling for a leg-up over the top. But when the tallest cat we have ever had, who, standing on his hind legs, now reaches a good three-quarters of the way up the chair-back before he even starts, *still* clambers babyishly up the carving, *still* bawls for help because he's stuck and

has, into the bargain, left a permanent trail of scratches over the acorns to mark his passage...

What, I sometimes ask, will they think of to ruin next? Why do they always pick on something that might one day, if they hadn't mucked it up, have been valuable? Why on earth, with all the experience we've had, do we go on having Siamese cats? Then I see Sass's blue eyes looking at me out of that anxious, pointed face – and I pick him up and hug him. That is my answer.

Two

Father Adams's standard comment when he looks at Sass is 'Theests 'ant 'alf got a rum 'un there.' Coming from the oldest and most omniscient of our neighbours, who never misses a thing that happens in the Valley and remembers our cats and their idiosyncrasies as far back as Sugieh's addiction to tracking down courting couples up on the hill, Solomon's belief as a kitten that he was a horse and the time Sheba got marooned up the telephone pole, that is saying something.

He is right, however. Rum Sass certainly is – in his appearance, in the things he does and in the uncanny way he has of looking at people. At first sight the intensity of his gaze strikes one as comical. At second glance one wonders. Who *is* the wiser – he or you? What does he know? What can he see? What is he thinking?

It is partly the shape of his face. Longer, narrower, with higher cheek-bones than any cat we have ever had, and a

chin so pointed he looks like an Elizabethan philosopher. 'Look at the length of his head,' his breeder sighs every time she sees him. 'If ever a cat was born to be a champion...'

He isn't one because, for all his Brain of Britain look, he got his tail bent as a kitten. Nobody knows how. He wasn't born like it. It isn't the now rarely seen throw-back Siamese kink which, when it does occur, is always towards the tip of the tail. At a month old he was perfect, his breeder Pauline Furber told us – then one day, suddenly, he appeared with this right-angled bend near the base. Whether he'd caught it in a door, or somebody had bitten it... certainly it couldn't have happened by itself. The Vet said the cartilage was damaged and it couldn't be splinted or operated on, being only a scant inch from his bottom. So there he was, the hope of the litter, with a tail like the starting-handle of a car.

It was at this point that we had rung Pauline Furber seeking a successor to Seeley, and she said she had just the kitten for us. He was an absolute character. Stuck out a mile from all the others. His only fault was that he had this bend in his tail...

I have told this part of the story before, too. How I discounted him at once. Our cats had always been perfect, I told her. It wouldn't seem right to see a crooked tail around the place. How we went, instead, to see the other kittens she had for sale – Saska's twin brother and four from a younger litter. Saska was there as companion to his brother – a role he'd so far fulfilled by hitting him in the eye. The younger kittens, however, were nowhere in the personality stakes next to Sass. His brother sat there with one eye shut like a woebegone small Lord Nelson. Guess who was swaggering

round like Superman, bent tail raised at triumph stations? Guess who we brought home with us that night, much to the disgust of our blue girl? Guess who is now her inseparable companion, the delight of our hearts – and the most noted cat in the district for his peculiarities?

We wouldn't have thought it possible. Our other cats, vigilant though we had always been with them, had nevertheless had a certain amount of freedom which enabled them to get into trouble. The daily look-round on their own before breakfast, for instance, which on occasion they extended to going half round the village, or the times when we took them for walks in the forest.

Mostly they followed at our heels but there had been times when they digressed. Up trees where they got stranded. After those courting couples. Vanishing suddenly into the undergrowth and worrying the daylights out of us. We'd call them, implore them, practically stand on our heads peering under brambles for them... afraid, if we left them, of people with guns or prowling foxes.

Somebody would usually happen by in due course to enquire what we were looking for and, being told a couple of Siamese cats, would inform us that there was one up that tree back there, or they'd just seen one go into our donkey field, or – as happened more than once – that there were two of them sitting right behind us. Would those be the ones? Though they didn't appear to be lost. They looked as if they'd been there for ages...

These days it was different. Since Seeley's disappearance Shebalu always wore a collar and lead when she was out. The lead was a twenty-foot nylon cord, admittedly, and didn't restrict her movements but one of us was always

there to grab it if she looked like taking off. Sass was too small for a collar yet. He'd have looked – being Sass he'd have undoubtedly seen to it that he did look – like a particularly hard-done-by cherub in a chain gang. In due course he, too, would have one. We couldn't risk losing a cat again. For the moment, though, there was no need. Like all young kittens he was nervous of the outside world and didn't want to venture far. His main concern was to keep close to us or Sheba.

Neither did there seem any need for a collar and lead when, as his legs began to lengthen like spindly brown pipe-cleaners, I started to take him up on the hillside behind the cottage. He was still a baby, crouching when a jay flew over; leaping spectacularly at butterflies, batting cautiously, pretending they were dangerous, at fir cones lying in the grass. Shebalu, full as only a Siamese female can be of the fact that she'd been Longer With Us than He Had, Hadn't She, and Knew This Hillside Better Than He Did, Didn't She? and anyway we Liked Her Better, sat by my side importantly, wearing her collar and lead as though they were an Egyptian queen's insignia, far too superior to play games with little kittens. So it was that I started throwing fir cones to give Saska something to chase after. Nobody was more surprised than I was when he picked them up and brought them back.

I threw them further away. Still he retrieved them – belting down the hillside with the speed of a greyhound and racing straight back up again carrying the cone in his mouth. He would put it down in front of me and watch it intently, ready to chase it again. It was always the exact one I'd thrown for him, too. If there were several lying around

when he got to the end of his run, he would sniff round like a police dog till he found the one that had the right scent on it. The only time he was ever foxed was when the cone bounced, on its way down, into the middle of a very large gorse bush. After circling the bush for ages with a worried look on his face, he eventually came back hopefully with a piece of donkey dropping.

While I thought Sass's retrieving act clever and encouraged him in it, there were some people who couldn't believe their eyes. Fred Ferry, Father Adams's perennial sparring partner, was the first outsider to see the performance as he clumped, knapsack over shoulder, along the lane one afternoon. From the way he stopped, watched incredulously for several minutes and then quickened his pace along the lane, I knew the news wouldn't be long in spreading and sure enough Father Adams appeared within seconds.

Father Adams knows us well enough by now not to bother with the usual village ploys when he wants to see what we are doing. No whistling a dog, washing mud off his gum boots in the stream that runs past the cottage or picking blackberries in our hedge for him. He just stands there, arms folded, and stares. He was there on that occasion when we came down at the end of the session and so saw the finale that Fred Ferry, not wanting to be thought lingering, had missed: Sass running ahead of me with his pine cone in his mouth, through the back gate, and putting it carefully down on the lawn.

'Well, if th'old liar weren't right for once,' said Father Adams. 'I 'ouldn't have believed it if I hadn't seen it for myself.' And off he went to add his bit to the story – about

our new cat carrying home things in his mouth like a retriever with a stick.

Alas, before long we had to give up the games on the hillside. It should have been safe. The area was fenced. We grazed Annabel, our donkey, up there. Beyond the fence was thick, untracked pine forest that nobody ever wandered through. It was well away from the bridle path, too, where I now never took the cats. In the old days we walked along the path often, but after the lesson of Seeley... Supposing, said Charles, I was halfway up the track with them and met a dog?

You can't win, of course. When it comes to being born to trouble as the sparks fly upwards, man has nothing on Siamese cats. There we were minding our own business up on the hillside one morning, Shebalu pursuing her favourite pastime of biting the heads off daisies, Sass busily occupied stalking beetles, Annabel grazing companionably close at hand to make sure she wasn't left out of anything, when out of the forest and through the top fence charged three large black Labradors.

It was like one of those animated dioramas. Shebalu went up a tree. Annabel took off across the hillside, bucking wildly in defence of her rear. She needn't have worried. Sass, an eye-catching target in his kitten whiteness, fled straight down the hillside towards the cottage, and the dogs, tongues lolloping, went after him.

So did I. So did Charles, running madly across from the orchard. So did the woman, frantically blowing a whistle, who came clambering over the fence in my rear. Charles reached the yard ahead of the Labradors and barred them from coming through the gate. Where was Sass, though –

conspicuous by his absence, last seen streaking like a comet down the hill?

Upstairs under our bed, as a matter of fact. I always leave the cottage doors open when I'm out with the cats – from past experience one never knows when they'll need a quick retreat. When we'd located him and satisfied ourselves that he wasn't hurt we went out to talk to the woman. We'd often seen her around before, instructing the dogs to sit in the roadway, walking on up the hill herself, then calling or whistling them to come on. Giving them obedience training, obviously, but what on earth she'd been doing in the woods...

Training them as gun dogs, according to her. She and her husband did a lot of it. The business out on the road was to get them to stay where they were put. The next step was to take them where there were likely to be distractions and teach them to still stay put till they were told. To this end she'd taken them into the forest, instructed them to 'sit' when a rabbit hopped out on to the path ahead—and the trio, deciding she couldn't possibly have meant it, had immediately shot off in pursuit. The rabbit must have given them the slip behind a tree and, pelting on, they'd spotted Sass.

'They wouldn't have hurt him,' the woman assured us with airy confidence. 'By instinct they retrieve without harming their quarry.' I don't know about that. I had a vision of Sass being carted back to her in one of those big black mouths and went weak at the knees. So it was that though she never brought the dogs to the Valley again – her confidence being obviously not as strong as she made out – for a long time I didn't take Sass up on the hill again, either. I never knew what might come out of the forest.

Instead I threw things for him to chase on the lawn – pine cones, pieces of stick and, as the summer advanced, small fallen apples from the tree in front of the conservatory. Sass himself devised the refinement to this one. If people's eyes popped to see him running back to me with sticks and fir cones, they positively goggled to see him carrying small apples by their stalks.

Fred Ferry, not ordinarily an animal lover, was entranced. 'Theest couldn't half train he to be useful,' he kept saying. As a poacher's assistant I imagined, knowing Fred, who didn't carry that knapsack for nothing. He was equally intrigued when I told him that Sass drank. Anything from orange juice to whisky.

Most Siamese like sherry, of course. One belonging to a friend of mine downed a whole glassful once. She put it on the floor by the side of her chair while she was having a quiet half-hour with the paper and when, after a while, she picked up the glass and found it empty she thought she must have drunk it without realising she had – until she saw the culprit weaving across the room with his legs crossed, just before he collapsed on the floor. Luckily her husband is a doctor. He said to lay him on the bed and leave him, and sure enough after an hour or two he recovered. If it had been us, we would have had to call the Vet. I can just imagine telling him one of our cats was drunk. That, I can hear him saying, is all he'd been waiting for...

With that example in mind, anyway, we always warn friends to watch their glasses. Siamese are forward enough without encouraging them in their drinking habits, and in any case it is bad for their kidneys. A finger-lick of sherry

is all our cats have ever been allowed – until Sass appeared on the scene and, almost before we knew it, there he was sitting persuasively on people's laps, bent tail at an angle behind him, hooking at their glasses with a determined paw and scoffing anything he could get.

Orange juice we don't mind about – though I have no doubt he thinks it's something stronger. People with more potent drinks are permitted to give him only a single finger-lick – and no more than two guests in an evening at that. Even so, from the way he sizes up the gathering, longing written all over him, one paw going out like a grab-hook for a practised yank at the glass, you'd think Charles and I kept Bacchanalia every night with that cat as one of the party. Actually we hardly drink at all. Seeing Sass, nobody would believe it.

Fred, as I say, was entranced when I told him about this. An ardent cider *aficionado* himself, he said Sass was a regular li'l wonder. I thought he was, too, watching him dashing about the lawn, diving head first into flower beds and nettles, retrieving apples with unerring accuracy and bringing them back to me like a dog. So much so that I got lax about always keeping close to him, Sass laid his plans accordingly, and one day, chasing an apple I'd tossed near the gate, he ran past it and over the wall.

He was across the road and up into the wood like a flash. So was I, in determined pursuit. But it took time to haul myself up the steep, slippery bank and by the time I'd got to the top he had vanished. Up through the trees I raced. How often had I done this chasing after Solomon. In those days, though, I could tell myself he always came back in the end. Now there was the frightening thought of Seeley.

I crashed through the wood, emerged on the lane at the top of the hill, went running past cottages and bungalows along to the end. There was no sign of him anywhere. No reply to my frantic calls. Only the sound of doors opening behind me as people came out to peer over their gates, and tap their heads at each other, I shouldn't wonder. Outside the Rose and Crown a thought came to me. Sass and his liking for drink. It was summer and the door was open. If he'd sniffed alcohol he might well have gone in.

Plucking up courage, I went in myself. 'I suppose a Siamese cat hasn't come in here?' I asked the gathering in general. Silence swept the bar in a sort of wave. The customers looked at me oddly. 'He's run away and he likes drink,' I said. The silence settled even deeper.

He obviously hadn't been there. I backed out, hot all over. Siamese land you in situations like that. I knew what those people were thinking. To add to my chagrin as I dashed back down to the Valley – the Forestry track being the next place to look for the truant – I suddenly saw him coming out of Fred Ferry's back door with Fred in attendance close behind.

Where had he been? In the Ferry kitchen, proving what I'd said about his drinking sherry. 'Walked in like he was the Squire and owned the place,' said Fred. 'I thought thee usn't mind if I give he a drop.'

Actually I did, but what was the use? 'Only give it to'n off me finger, like theest said,' Fred assured me. And Sass had licked his finger with enthusiasm and stood on his hind legs and sniffed hopefully at the bottle.

When Fred told that one up at the Rose and Crown – in which direction he departed as soon as Sass and I left him

– the customers would realise I'd had some reason for thinking he might be there, but I bet they still put me down as barmy.

Three

There was one consolation. Charles and I were no longer considered the village's sole eccentrics. We had strong competition from the Bannetts.

I have mentioned them before. Tim with his ginger beard. His wife Liz, who wore long skirts and dangling earrings. Their family of tortoises and turtles who each slept in a bedroom slipper in front of the sitting-room fire. They'd moved into the cottage next to Miss Wellington and were by this time living the rural life in earnest. Not as we do, simply because we like it and would hate a town existence. They are of the conviction, popular among the young, that when civilisation falls apart – they expect it to happen daily – the only solution will be to live off the land and they might as well get in training for it.

They began by keeping chickens and bees. Tim being of an artistic as well as a practical bent, the chickens were not

as other people's chickens. They were exotics – Oricanas and Marrons, funny little birds with ruffs and topknots, who laid arsenic-green and bitter-chocolate coloured eggs, which the locals immediately decided must be poisonous. Actually they were delicious, but only we and the Bannetts ate them. The rest of the village regarded them as akin to toadstools.

The bees were normal bees, but people who keep bees always seem odd somehow. They wear strange clothes, for instance – in Tim's case a white boiler suit topped with a wide-brimmed yellow straw hat in which, with a black veil hanging from it, draped around his beard, he looked like a Victorian butterfly-collector bound for the Amazon or the Reverend Dodgson off on a picnic with Alice long ago.

Bee-keepers do odd things, too. In Tim's case the two pictures which come most outstandingly to mind are of him standing in his bee-outfit in the lane one morning apparently rooted to the spot, saying 'Ow! Ow! Ow!' to himself in a voice that was muted yet fraught with anguish (he later explained that he'd been trying not to antagonise still further some bees that had got through a hole in his boiler suit and were stinging him, but they were obviously antagonised enough already so he gave up and went home at the double)... and of his lying on a chaise longue in his garden one day, right in front of the bee-hive, wearing only denim shorts and with a swelling bee-sting on his nose.

He was, as is the case with most people's garden activities round here, in full view over the wall.

'Now I've seen the lot,' said Father Adams, after he'd walked past specially to take a look.

'Sure he ain't dead?' asked Fred Ferry, always out for a sensation.

'Thee dussn't half have 'em round here,' opined the third member of our Hear All, See All, Tell All brigade, Ern Biggs, who, by virtue of his working as an odd-job man in our village but living in a neighbouring one, attributes anything that happens here to the fact that, as a village, we're all peculiar.

Actually Tim was lying there combining a much-needed rest from his self-sufficiency activities – up at dawn to feed the chickens, hoeing potatoes, grinding wheat by hand for Liz to make home-made bread – with an experiment into the theory of gaining better results from bees by communicating trust and friendship to them. Some people do it by talking to them. Tim was endeavouring to do it by thought transference. He obviously hadn't transferred much trust so far since one of the guard bees had stung him on the nose, but one had to give him full marks for trying.

'Why han't he got no clothes on?' enquired Ern Biggs when the motive was explained to him – but there was a reason for the bathing shorts, too. Bees, Tim explained, were angered by the smell of sweat. This way he wouldn't get so heated.

All very well, but the village had its eye on him and when it came to the goats...

Goat-keeping might well be described as the buttress of self-sufficiency, provided one has the space. They supply their owners with milk, cheese, yoghurt – even butter if one can stand the taste. Many people buy a goat in milk and start out that way. Tim and Liz began the other way round. They arranged to buy a female kid – the offspring of

a goat belonging to some other self-sufficiency enthusiasts – which they proposed to have at six weeks old, rear by hand till it could look after itself, mate at the end of a year and so go into the goat business gradually.

They prepared a small house and yard, put up a hayrack and feeding trough, bought a collar, chain and tethering pin. We thought it overdoing things a bit when, invited to inspect the preparations, we saw a milking-stool and stainless steel can hanging in readiness from the ceiling, but apparently that is one of the tenets of self-sufficiency. Buy now, while things are still about. By the time civilisation does fall apart there won't be a milking-stool or can to be had. They'll all be lying stacked in other people's goat houses and you'll have to barter for them with sacks of turnips.

It was also, said Tim, with an air of practicality, to show the kid from the start what was expected of her. There could be no room for sentiment in survivalism. She must produce milk at the earliest possible moment – *and* her proper quota – or goat's meat would be the order of the day.

We knew better than that, and sure enough the day came when the breeders brought the young kid over. Not to leave her – that was still more than a week away, but for a visit, with her mother, by way of introduction. The Bannetts rang us excitedly. They'd bring her down to the Valley so we could see her, they said, and in due course the procession appeared. Tim and the man, both with patriarchal beards and in clothes that looked suitably rural. Liz and the man's wife in the long skirts and cloaks that young people these days affect. A couple of children frolicked on ahead. Tim was encouraging a minute black and white kid to walk beside

him. There was no sign of the mother goat. Presumably this was an experimental solo outing.

They went past the cottage looking like a rural scene by Constable and I called to Charles to come and watch. Obviously they were going for a stroll up the Valley and would call on us on the way back. I was just commenting what a picture they made when there was a sudden commotion in the ranks. Back up the hill shot the little kid with Tim running like mad behind her.

It seemed that Tim, our idealist, had refused to put her on a lead saying he wanted her to follow him from affection. She'd trotted along with the nice man for a while but then the thought of Mum, back on the Bannetts' lawn, had been too strong. She was bounding back up now in spectacularly curving leaps, the height of which beat even Saska's. Tim did a spectacular leap himself in an attempt to grab her, but slipped and fell flat on his face. Up he got. On the pair of them went. The rest of the party waited at the bottom. Eventually he came back carrying her, having caught up with her at the cottage.

We went out to look at her. She was an entrancing little thing. Long-legged, pale-eyed, about the size of a Siamese cat, with hooves like polished thimbles and a coat like astrakhan. 'Whass be going to do with she?' asked Father Adams, appearing as if through a trapdoor on .the scene. '*Keep* her?' he echoed, as if he hadn't heard aright. 'Whass be goin' to feed her on, then?'

It was a question that Tim must have asked himself often during the weeks which followed. They called her Polly. Within a week she'd eaten all the foliage in the Bannetts' garden – there wasn't much spare space there anyway

what with the bees, the goat house and a couple of chicken runs – and, notwithstanding concentrates, hay and regular milk-feeds they gave her, something had to be done about providing her with greenery.

Tim seemed to be everywhere with that one small goat. Hovering on the hill with her on a lead while she avidly cropped down the verges. Frantically cutting waste grass with a scythe and toting it back for Liz to feed her during the day. 'Some people don't half look for work,' said Father Adams. 'If theest ask I, t'ould be cheaper to buy a pinta.'

They still were buying it, of course. Plus the concentrates. Plus hay. Plus special powdered milk which had to be made up, warmed to the right temperature and bottle-fed to her at regular intervals. Tim was as fussy about this as a first-time mother over baby feeds. Liz had a timetable as to what to do during the day. So had we when, on the rare occasions when they took time off – usually to go to a farm sale to buy implements that were years out of date, or old-fashioned crocks for Liz's cooking – we fed and shut the chickens in for them and were given the honour of looking after Polly.

The chickens were easy save for having to go into the runs crouched down like King Kong. Tim had adapted the old earth closet (boarded over at the top to half its height) as a roosting hut for one lot and a large wooden cider barrel for the other. The runs were in front of these and, owing to Tim having acquired a bargain lot of chicken-wire which was only three feet wide, that was the height of the runs and the difficulty was obvious.

Not so much to Tim perhaps, who was used to it and in any case always closed the huts at dusk. But to Charles, six feet tall, venturing bent double into one of the runs to shut

the door of the barrel... while it was still quite light because the door was a peculiar shape and he wanted to see what he was doing... 'Whass be up to now then?' came the inevitable question over the wall. Charles, turning to answer, collided with one of the random poles that supported the roof-wire, and before my own and Father Adams's very eyes the run collapsed on the floor.

That was a minor incident, however. It was Polly who presented the biggest problem. If the Bannetts were going to be away for more than a few hours they brought her down to us, together with the number of feeding-bottles necessary to keep her going till they returned; a small bowl of concentrates with which, when it was her going-home time, we were supposed to entice her up the hill; her chain; a two-foot-long tethering pin shaped like a giant corkscrew; and a list of instructions as long as my arm.

'Be sure the pin is screwed right down to the base in the ground – you'd be surprised how strong she can be', was one. 'Make sure the milk is warmed to blood heat and don't let her suck air', was another.

A chance would have been a fine thing. The moment that goat saw her milk-feed coming she was at it like a commando on an assault course. She made a jump for it, went backwards tugging like a rope-puller on it – I had a job to keep hold of the bottle. I had no chance to expel the air before she got at it and it wouldn't have made much difference if I had. She gulped in so much round the sides, sucking away like a corporation drain-clearer, it was a wonder she didn't blow up and float off.

She survived though. Goats are obviously tougher than text-book writers imagine. She even appeared to like us.

When Tim brought her down to the Valley to graze along the verges she'd start running as soon as she saw us. Hard down the road, trailing her lead, Tim following indulgently behind. She didn't bother about the gate. She came over the wall and rushed at us, ecstatically wagging her tail. Wasn't it *wonderful*, enthused Miss Wellington, how that dear little animal adored us?

To a degree it was, but it didn't do the wall much good. It is dry-stone built and easily falls down. If Annabel was on the lawn, too – she didn't like Polly at all – Polly would put her head down and pretend-butt at Annabel. Annabel would turn her rear to kicking position. A pair of warning legs jutted backwards like the ready-cocked hammers of a shotgun – we were always having to jump in hastily to whip Polly out of firing range.

It was no easier if the cats were with us. Shebalu crouched, crossed her eyes and growled like a tiger while Sass took up attack position. Back arched like a hairpin, tail bushed like a flue brush, he advanced sideways at her on long stiff legs with his head down, like a crab. The effect was somewhat spoiled by his tail sticking out at the wrong angle but there was no doubt that our dark man meant business. Tim would grab Polly's collar, I would pick up Saska – who would immediately take advantage of this to start up the most blood-curdling howling. Lucky for her I was holding him Back, he would announce from the safety of my shoulder. If he was down on the ground right now – gosh, he wouldn't half Fight.

He might have done at that. He is the most fearless cat we have ever had, though whether it is innate bravery or thick-headedness we can't determine. Certainly neither

the cats nor Annabel would have countenanced our having a goat of our own, though we liked Polly so much there were times when we thought of it. Only fleetingly, however. Something always seemed to happen to bring home the disadvantages of goat-keeping. Like the time we might have been arrested, had the public been more observant.

It was, as I remember, one day in February. Tim and Liz were going to be away for the afternoon. They might be a little late back, said Tim. It would be all right for Polly to be in her yard till it got dark. But could we lock her in, and give her her bottle, around half-past five?

Of course we could. Normally I would have heated the bottle in the kitchen and just carried it up the hill. That afternoon, however, we had to go to town to get a car battery, as our current one was patently failing. It was a dismal day and I shrank at the thought of coming home, heating the feed and taking it up the hill again in the cold. It was then that I had my idea.

It was, quite simply, to take a thermos of boiling water, the cats' hot water bottle and Polly's feed with us in the car. Before we left town I would fill the hot water bottle from the thermos, wrap it against the feeding-bottle in a car rug... in the half-hour it took to get back to the village Polly's bottle would warm up nicely and we could nip in and feed her before we drove on down the hill.

Why didn't I save all that trouble and just put the heated feed in the thermos? Because Charles is particular about germs. Goodness only knew what the composition of the goat-feed was, he said when I suggested it. He didn't want it in a thermos he was likely to drink from.

Fair enough. Showing considerable forethought, in fact. Where we slipped up was that neither of us remembered Polly's bottle before we left town and we were half way home before I thought of it. I yelled to Charles to stop. He immediately pulled in at the roadside. Carefully I filled the hot water bottle. OK now, I said, having wrapped it against the feeding-bottle in the car rug. It would be just about right when we got home. At which point Charles pulled the self-starter and nothing happened. The battery had completely given out.

'It could be worse,' said Charles, trying to look on the bright side. 'At least we've got the new one in the boot.' Then he peered sideways out of the window. 'Great Scott!' he said. 'Do you realise where we've *stopped?*'

Outside the local RAF station and it was at the time of the bomb scares. It couldn't have happened to anybody but us.

I can see us now. Me shining a dimming torch into the boot while Charles lifted out a black, rectangular object. Cars catching us in their headlights by the dozen while he carried it round to the front. Putting it down by the offside wheel where it managed to look most sinister. And of course the most traumatic moment of all, when he disconnected the old battery and all the lights on the car went out. We must have looked like Guy Fawkes and his assistant, flitting about in the dark, both bonnet and boot of the car up and a black box standing in the road. Any moment we expected to hear the sirens of police cars, or a bugle calling out the RAF guard at the double.

Charles tightened the connections like greased lightning. We were in and on our way home as if jet-propelled. So

much that we forgot to stop on our way down the hill and had to walk up with Polly's feed after all.

'Everything all right?' asked Tim when he rang later to thank us. Even he could hardly credit it when I told him.

Four

There were times – just occasionally, when Annabel happened for once to be out of sight around the corner, not watching us like a police-check from up on the hill; when the cats were indoors sleeping the sleep of the contented and there was no goat perched like a mountain chamois on our wall – when the cottage looked as somnolent and non-eventful as if time had passed it by for a hundred years.

I was working in the garden one such afternoon, battering away with a fork with one prong missing at a flower bed that was as hard as iron, my mind churning busily over various problems, when a woman came meandering along the lane.

She was acting like a RADA student making her first attempt at Ophelia. Breaking off branches, holding them in the air and tilting her head at them, stooping to pick up bits

of moss which she placed carefully in a basket. She added a piece of stone and looked to see if I was watching. 'I collect these,' she informed me brightly.

That being obvious, I just said, 'Oh.' Presumably I was supposed to ask why. Deciding, as I didn't, that my horizons needed extending, she came over to the cottage gate.

She couldn't understand, she said in the course of conversation, why, just because they lived in the country, women seemed to let themselves *go*. Not just the way they *dressed*. (I had on a sagging sweater with holes in it. She was wearing a hat with feathers and a matching coat.) But *mentally*. *Intellectually*. There were other things than cleaning the house and digging the garden.

Women owed it to themselves to expand their potential, she went on. Men appreciated them all the more. She herself did Japanese flower arranging. Had I any interest like that?

Well no, I said. I didn't have time... One should *make* time for culture, she reproved me. There was no need for anyone to turn into a cabbage... She would come and see me again.

She drifted on up the lane, picking an odd-shaped branch here, a sad-looking seedhead there, hard at work being a floral artist. Fred Ferry told me later that she'd just moved out from town. I wondered... should I have enlightened her?

The broken fork, for instance, which her glance had dismissed as slovenly – that had history behind it. Charles had snapped the tine off years before, despatching an adder which had threatened the cats. Actually it was more useful with only three prongs; it fitted more easily between the

plants. The flower bed was like concrete not on account of neglect, but because two cats, a donkey and a goat kept prancing over it. As for the faraway expression I wore – it had nothing to do with being bored. As a matter of fact I'd been thinking about Sass. Wondering what made him tick.

We were always wondering that. There'd been the instance, a few days after his arrival, when Shebalu introduced him to grass. She'd loathed him to begin with, but now he'd begun to take on the smell of the cottage and she'd decided he wasn't too bad. So out she'd gone, sniffing a Daisy She Owned here, chattering at a Bird Who Was Frightened Of Her there, greeting Charles with a matey 'Waaaah' as she and Sass passed him – and, by the garage, at a clump she'd always favoured, stopping to eat Her Grass.

Never had she chewed it so appreciatively, head on one side, eyes closed in satisfaction. Delicious, she announced. Been eating it for Years and Years. Nobody but her ate This Grass.

They did now. Sass, having adopted her as his Mum and mentor, which meant faithfully copying everything she did, put his head down as near to her as he could get and started to chew it as well. There was a look of earnest owlishness on his face we were soon to learn to recognise. It meant that Sass was thinking. In this case presumably why big cats ate grass and deciding it must be on account of its colour. That was the only reason we could think of why from that time on he ate everything he came across that was green.

Cabbages, brussels sprouts, watercress – he chewed industriously away at the lot. He smelt like Covent Garden, but we told ourselves it was doing him good. I remember the watercress particularly – I'd bought it to garnish a duck

one day when we were having friends to supper, and when I nipped into the village shop for another bunch just on closing time, explaining that Sass had eaten the first... 'He ate the *watercress*?' echoed the proprietor in a voice that was loud with astonishment. 'Wasn't he interested in the *duck*?' The heads of the other customers swivelled like lightning. They thought I was talking about Charles. I explained about Sass liking green stuff, however, which they accepted as reasonably credible... One woman said she knew of a cat that ate cucumber. Another had a dog that liked rhubarb. A day or two later the first one turned up at the cottage bringing a bunch of watercress for Sass as a present.

I invited her in and let her give it to him herself. I couldn't think what else *to* do. How, after what I'd said in good faith in the shop, could I have told her the truth? That he'd now got an obsession about green plastic netting and had abandoned fresh greenstuff for that?

I might as well have done. You should have seen the look on her face when he backed, ears flat, away from the watercress. Trying to feed him that stuff, he wailed. She think he was potty or something?

Obviously she now thought I was, and we were sure he was, which probably made some sort of equation. Even allowing for Siamese being different, however, his passion for netting was most odd.

It started with our bringing home a half-hundredweight of onions in a green plastic sack which we'd bought at the local Saturday market. We'd happened to meet Tim Bannett there and he'd just bought two sacks himself. Next year, when he was better organised, he told us, he was going to grow his own. Meanwhile, as the next best thing, he was

buying them in bulk. Liz was going to string these like the
Breton onions – it told you how in the self-sufficiency book
and they'd look good hanging up near the jars of honey.
With their home-made wine on the shelves, he added, and
the box of apples we'd given them... There was a sort of
Virginian pioneer's Thanksgiving look on his face.

There was one on Charles's, too, as we also drove home
with a sack of onions. Tim was right, he enthused. The big
porch outside the kitchen, which we'd recently had built to
take gum boots and anoraks and the freezer, would make an
admirable winter store. A couple of sacks of potatoes; one of
flour; these onions; his cob-nuts when he harvested them.
There was something in this self-sufficiency business – it
gave one an independent, let-'em-all-come feeling.

It did indeed. I began to have visions myself. Big stone
jars of pickles; a neatly-stacked winter woodpile – not the
last-minute odds and ends we frenziedly sawed up now.
Perhaps we could get one of those big pine dressers for the
kitchen, I said. I rather liked them. It would go well with
our red-tiled floor and the strings of onions. We had our old
oil-lamps, too, which we'd used before we got electricity at
the cottage. I could get those out and polish them. They'd
look really right on the dresser.

So long as I didn't want to actually use them, said Charles.
We'd had enough of groping round in dimness before. He
had other things to do this winter.

So, dreaming our dreams, we drove home with our sack of
onions and stacked it proudly against the wall in the porch
– only to find Sass chewing at the mesh a few minutes later
as if it was his one hope of getting to Mecca.

It couldn't have been the smell of the netting which attracted him. That was over-powered by the onions. It wasn't the onions either. When I offered him one he ignored it. It was then that it struck me it might be the colour of the netting – green like the grass and the watercress. Experts say cats are colour-blind and see only in shades of grey. I wondered, though – could Sass be different? It was a theory I put to Charles a few days later after an incident in the orchard.

By this time, worried by Saska's preoccupation with the sack (Charles having come up with the thought that the dye in the netting might be poisonous), we'd moved it up to the spare-room-cum-study as the one place our gannet couldn't get at it. I write up there, it is a very small room and the smell of onions is hardly like that of violets – but, as Charles said, which was more important? Sass, indubitably. I put up with the onions.

So this particular day I was upstairs working, Charles was in the orchard, Shebalu was asleep downstairs (four years older than Sass, she insists on senior rights occasionally) and Sass, bereft of company, was busy bawling the place down. I could tell by the rise and fall of the howling that he was wandering from room to room. Presently there was silence. A creak on the stairs. I waited for it – the sound of sniffing at the door jamb. Then the hiatus which I knew from long experience with Siamese meant he was peering under the door.

His bellow when it came was like the foghorn on the Lizard. He knew I was In There! he roared. He could See Me! Why didn't I Let Him In? What was in there he wasn't supposed to know about?

I could stand the foghorn. I'd had long experience of that, too. What I couldn't stand was when he started chewing the carpet. I carried him over to Charles who said of course he'd have him in the orchard – he was so intelligent he was always a delight to be with. 'Couldn't she be bothered with you then?' I heard him ask as the two of them made their way up through the gooseberry patch. Sass gave a man-to-man 'Wow!'

I went back to my work. For a while all was peace and silence, then I heard footsteps thumping up the stairs. It was Charles, clutching Sass. His face was scarlet. Did I know, he said, what this cat of mine had done? Gone straight up an apple tree – right to the top – and chewed a whacking great hole in the net!

The apple trees are netted to keep off the birds, whom we like but who devastate our crops. The nets are expensive and Charles had spent ages putting them on, manoeuvring them carefully with a pole to cover all the branches. Admittedly this was autumn and the birds wouldn't start in till the spring, but 'A brand new net!' groaned Charles. 'And now I've got to take a ladder up and mend the hole with string. That blasted cat must be bonkers.'

It was then I pointed out that the nets were green, like the onion sack and the watercress. Perhaps he was a breakthrough, I said; a cat who recognised colour. Charles said breakthrough was the right description for him, the way he'd gone through that fruit net. But why should he get fanatical about things that were *green*, not brown or white or blue?

Maybe when he saw Shebalu eating her grass clump with such reverence, I said, he thought he should eat everything

that colour to be on the safe side. Maybe it was some sort of Siamese ritual, like that business of his with the rug. (The rug is a story with many facets. I'd better tell that one later.) The more I saw of Sass, I confessed, I wondered whether he was superstitious.

Charles looked at the cat we were talking about. Sass never wasted time. Having done his stuff with green netting for the day he was obviously practising for his next encounter with Polly. Back arched, tail stuck out like a teacup handle, he was advancing across the room at absolutely nothing. He stiffened, feinted, jumped aside, spun round... advanced sideways at nothing again. He didn't know about superstitious, said Charles. If I asked him, that cat was nuts.

Five

We first realised we had a strain of unusual mice in the Valley when we were returning from a walk one day with Annabel.

I was in front, going ahead to open the Forestry gate, Charles was coming behind with his four-legged girlfriend, when what I thought was an autumn leaf skittered across the track in front of me and came to rest at the bottom of the bank. It moved again as I got near it and I saw that it was a field-mouse. Chestnut brown, small – the size of a half-grown oak leaf – and making no attempt whatever to get away. Maybe it was injured, I thought, stooping to pick it up and put it where Annabel wouldn't tread on it. (I'll pick up anything with gloves on except an adder; another thing I've grown used to over the years.)

It wasn't injured, however. It was sitting up on its haunches eating grass seed, turning the tassel like a corn-

cob in incredibly tiny paws, ignoring me completely as if I were some sort of local tree. By the time Charles came up it had finished that grass head and moved a foot or so up the bank, where it selected another which it sat up and nibbled while it looked interestedly down at Annabel.

'Perhaps it's got concussion,' I whispered to Charles. Never had I seen an outdoor mouse so confident. Charles studied it closely.

'Nothing wrong with that one,' he said. 'It's just not afraid of anything.'

Neither was the one I saw next day eating bird crumbs by the cotoneaster in the yard. It was sitting nonchalantly with its back to me and didn't even turn round as I passed. It wasn't the mouse we'd seen in the lane. This one was definitely larger. There was the same air of insouciance, however – the obvious lack of fear. I wondered if they came from the same litter.

That afternoon the cotoneaster mouse was taken into custody by Shebalu. I shouted when I saw her creeping up on him but he determinedly took no notice. She carried him indoors, moaning horribly between her teeth as is her wont when she's announcing that she's caught something. That in itself would frighten most mice to death – it shakes even me when I hear it. But the moment she put it down to give a louder bellow for Sass (never around, said her expression, when he was Wanted) the mouse got up and, while she still had her mouth open, nipped quietly into the kitchen.

I hoped he'd go straight through it and out into the yard but instead he went into a cupboard. Not, we realised when we knew him better, because he was scared and seeking

refuge. He was busy summing up the prospects. That was in October. That mouse, soon to be known as Lancelot (because, phonetically, that was what he did to Charles's nuts), stayed with us till the following spring, resisting all our attempts to expel him. He moved his headquarters at times but we always knew where he was. We had only to look for the cats.

It was they, the first day, who told us he was in the cupboard. They were camped hopefully outside it. Sass with not the least idea why he was there – he'd never yet seen a mouse – but copying Shebalu, trying to look intent, though his ears did wander occasionally. I shut them in the living-room and turned out the tins and packets. Sure enough there was the mouse in the last corner. I put on a glove, reached out a hand – he jumped over it and disappeared behind me.

He was under the cooker, according to Shebalu, whom I fetched out to say where he'd gone. *He* could actually See Him, said Sass, peering under with one eye. Apparently the mouse saw Saska, too. He shot out and into another cupboard. Only to check that he had an escape route, though. Having done so he came back and went under the cooker.

There, shuttling between cooker and cupboard with the waste bin sheltering his passage (we put it there on purpose to give him protection from the cats) he lived contentedly for several days and might indeed have spent all winter... there were only cleaning things in that cupboard and I kept the doors of the others firmly closed... if it weren't for the fact that I began to have a conscience about him. It seemed hardly the life for a field-mouse.

I started to put down crumbs for him. They were definitely gone each morning. After a couple of days, though, I had another thought. What could he be getting to drink? I put down a saucer of water and he certainly made use of that. From the splashings on the floor next morning he'd either fallen in it or had a bath.

He was obviously happy now, the only snag being that we had to keep the cats out of the kitchen in case they caught him. Not only was it difficult – sometimes I wondered if they got through the door by thought transference, the way I'd be sure I'd shut them on one side only to find them next minute on the other – but also it didn't seem fair. Sass in particular adored the kitchen. He couldn't get up to the work-tops yet, owing to his inability to jump, but he liked to sit out there and savour the smells and think about what I might be going to give him next.

Ergo, one night I laid a trail of crumbs out to the porch and put Lancelot's water saucer out there as well. That he'd transferred headquarters was confirmed next morning when the cats went straight to the refrigerator. He was Under There, said Shebalu, putting her nose to the bottom. Eating, Sass solemnly informed us, putting his nose down there as well. He was indeed. Lancelot had found El Dorado. Charles's harvest of cob-nuts.

Charles had brought them in and put them in the porch in a big plastic bin with its lid off, so that any damp would evaporate and not rot them. I had wondered about mice at the time, but he said they couldn't climb the bin-sides. What he hadn't reckoned with, however, was that Lancelot was no ordinary mouse. Not for him trying futilely to climb the plastic. He'd gone up the leg of the table we had out there and

launched himself downwards into the bin. To get out again, of course, he had only to drop off over the edge, the bin being filled to the top. Judging from the trail of nuts leading to the refrigerator he'd been working a transfer system all night.

Charles was so impressed he said he was welcome to share the nuts. He certainly was a clever little chap, getting away from Shebalu like that and proving himself so resourceful. Which wasn't what he said when he looked at his duffel coat one day (we'd noticed the cats had been sniffing suspiciously below it) and discovered that while Lancelot might eat nuts under the refrigerator by day, that certainly wasn't where he spent his nights. He'd chewed big holes in the duffel, carried the resultant wool into one of the pockets, and constructed a neat, soft bed suspended on the wall, safe from frost and patrolling cats.

It wasn't what I said either, a week or two after that, when Lancelot and Charles between them caused chaos at the cottage.

It began with our buying a caravan. Why we bought it I will explain later. As you may guess, it was connected with the cats. Suffice it for the moment to say that we'd bought a second-hand caravan – in November because it was then that we saw the one we wanted. We'd been looking for one since September and this was the first one that fitted the bill. And because it was in superb condition and had until then been kept undercover in the winter, Charles said we would keep it undercover too. A little beauty like that deserved it, he said, patting it affectionately on the side. When I puzzledly enquired where, he said the shed next to Annabel's stable. My heart sank with a thud when I heard it. You should just have seen that shed!

We'd owned it for nearly twenty years and from the moment we'd bought it, along with the orchard, Charles had used it as a store for things that might one day come in handy. Not things of any value, like the heavy roller, for instance, which we'd used once in twenty years and was kept in the garage. (Charles was always saying This Spring he'd roll the lawn, but somehow he never got round to it.)

No. The shed, which was open-fronted, contained a sort of magpie's nest of bits and pieces. The load of stone removed when we had the fireplace opened up, for instance. (Charles had said it would cost a fortune to buy that lot; we'd be glad of it for repairing the walls.) Earth excavated when we had the extension put on the cottage; according to Charles it was good topsoil. (Dump it in the shed, he'd told the builder at the time; later he'd spread it on the garden.) Soot, stored undercover to keep it from being de-natured by the rain. The remains of a load of mushroom compost, left there for the same purpose. Bags of sand. A mêlée of metal poles and wire, which we'd once used as an enclosure for Annabel and had never been able to untangle.

Somewhere in the depths was an old-fashioned folding bed-spring Charles had destined, years before, for a garden frame. In one corner were several reserve sacks of coal, hidden behind an old door. Eight heavy scaffolding planks were stacked at the rear – we'd used them to whitewash the cottage that summer. Surmounting everything else, the top of the magpie's nest, was our winter supply of kindling. Apple-tree prunings, sycamore branches, put there diligently by Charles. One reached it by standing on a convenient mound of earth there hadn't been room for inside. To stop the kindling cascading down, which it tended to do when

one tried to pull out a piece, it was held in place by loops of rope fastened to the crossbeam at random intervals. 'Nonsense,' said Charles, when I complained that it looked like Steptoe's yard. That's part of country living.'

Now he was suggesting clearing it and I should have jumped for joy. Being me, I was worrying about what we were going to do with it. 'Absolutely nothing to it,' said Charles. 'We'll have it cleared in half a day.'

Maybe so if we'd hired a bulldozer and put that lot where it deserved, on the local rubbish tip. But Charles insisted on removing it bit by bit, as if we were delving for jewels. Ten bags of manure – you'd have thought they were jewels, the reverence with which he carted them away. Must have matured for years, he said. They'd be worth their weight in gold on the rhubarb.

Coal to the conservatory. Kindling to Annabel's stable. She snuffed and snorted at it with displeasure. Stacking That Stuff in Her Place, she said... she wasn't going to have Those Planks. She did have them, propped across the back of her stable wall, and snorted her annoyance all the louder, banging her feeding bowl about at night to show what little space she now had. There was enough room in there for six donkeys, Charles told her, and it would keep her much warmer in winter.

It needed to. It was the coldest winter we'd had in years and it took us a fortnight to clear that shed. Lugging out the stones, cold enough to have come from a glacier, pickaxing the solid heaps of earth, trundling it off in a barrow with ice-cold handles whose frozen wheel would hardly turn. Normally we would have had plenty of assistance, but for some reason all our neighbours seemed to have been

suddenly struck with palsy. Tim Bannett had flu. Father Adams had arthritis – it had come on when we told him about clearing the shed. As for Fred Ferry, he'd come past the first morning, clumping stolidly along as is his wont. 'Whass doin' in there?' he'd stopped to enquire, and when we'd told him he looked astounded and said 'Never!'

'Thought theest was leaving that lot for they blokes what digs up the past,' he said. Fred prides himself on his subtle sense of humour. When I suggested maybe he could help us – we'd pay him at the usual rates – I fancied the humour faded slightly, but he said 'Ah. I'll see. I'll let thee know,' and trudged on up the hill. When he came down again he was limping too. He said his knee trouble had suddenly cropped up again. It always does when Fred needs an excuse. We knew when we were beaten.

So we toiled on. Up in the morning. Out on the job. Our labours seemed absolutely endless. At one stage Charles nearly joined the rest of them in our village of limping men. We'd got down to the layer where the bed-spring was and he incautiously walked across it. I warned him I could see a space underneath and that the spring appeared to be propped up on boxes. He wouldn't listen. Before my very eyes one of his legs went down through the spring and he was stuck like Long John Silver. If I hadn't been there to grab him when he sank, goodness knows what might have happened. As it was he emerged with only a scraped ankle – and if you are wondering what this had to do with Lancelot, it was the morning after this that, inadvertently, he and Charles produced their combined operation.

Charles, when we were working on clearing the shed, always locked the cottage doors. Quite right, too. As he

said, we were out of sight and earshot. Any passing stranger could walk in. Charles being punctilious, it involved removing two keys – the Yale one belonging to the old back door, which was now the inner door of the extension, and the key to the new outer extension door, which was of the ordinary non-Yale type. That one was simple. The key had to be outside before you could lock it. It was the inner door you had to watch. You had to remember to bring the Yale key with you before you shut it or you could find yourself locked out.

Normally that key stayed in the inner door all day, but with one of us now removing it constantly, tensed up with all the work we were doing, feeling like a couple of hard-pressed navvies – that morning, thinking I was accompanying him and had the key in my pocket, Charles banged the inner door shut. I hadn't got the key. I was merely shaking out the breakfast cloth. We were now completely locked out. And in the moment of silence in which we stood there, taking in what we had done, I suddenly realised I could hear Lancelot chewing noisily away behind the freezer.

He was always chewing noisily. At Charles's cob-nuts, under the refrigerator. He worked away like a nutmeg grater all day. But behind the freezer... was he at the electricity wires? If so, at any moment it could catch on fire!

I shouted for Charles, who was in the tool-house hunting for a hammer to break a window. It was the only way to get into the kitchen again and Charles wasn't very pleased about it. Unfortunately when I called to him about Lancelot he put down the rake he'd been holding and it slipped and smashed a stack of flowerpots. Well anyway, he hadn't used those for ages, I consoled him – but Charles was by this

time beyond consoling. He strode into the porch, seized the corner of the freezer... 'Mind we don't squash Lancelot,' I said. Charles told me what he'd like to do to Lancelot, but I noticed he moved it carefully all the same.

Halfway through, Lancelot emerged and went under a cupboard. He hadn't been chewing the wires. It must just have been that he fancied a change of residence. Under the freezer was a fresh pile of Charles's nuts. We gathered them up, replaced the freezer, pulled out the refrigerator and swept the heap of nutshells from underneath that. If we cleared that out for him perhaps he'd go back there and *stay* there, said Charles. When he was under there we at least knew what he was doing.

Charles smashed the window. I climbed through. We patched it temporarily with cardboard so the cats couldn't get out. Swept up the glass. Retrieved the key. Marched back to our private Siberia in the caravan shed. Did I ever stop to think, enquired Charles, what animals got us into? We wouldn't have thought of a caravan if it hadn't been for the cats. We wouldn't have been out here slaving. If we hadn't encouraged Lancelot he wouldn't have got into mischief under the freezer. And he, Charles, wouldn't have broken the flowerpots.

We wouldn't have had to hire a couple of ten-foot jacks, either, to hold up the shed roof when we found one of the support poles was rotten. We wouldn't have had to ring the Forestry Commission in a panic asking if they could supply us, quickly, with a pole. Alas, they had no spare poles, and no men available to cut one. The Forester asked if we could possibly fell one ourselves. It was the best he could do to help us, he said. He'd send us an invoice in due course.

It almost came to that. All it needed to complete the picture would have been Charles and me sawing down one of the Forestry pine trees while the village looked on wondering what on earth we were doing. Half an hour later, however, the Forester rang us back to say that a couple of his men had just come in. He was sending them over right away. It would be safer than our felling a tree ourselves. He hadn't felt too happy about that. Neither had we, and in fact in the meantime a neighbour had offered us a spare pole that *he* had and we'd accepted it – the only snag being that I'd left Charles holding it up like Atlas while I'd dashed down to answer the phone.

Eventually the shed was ready. The caravan went halfway in and immediately had to be pulled out again. Its rooflight was touching the crossbeam and we didn't want it broken. There were plenty of hands to help us now, however. It was like the launching of a ship. All the hard work done. Just a gentle heave from our audience after Charles had climbed the ladder and planed the crossbeam.

Fred Ferry hauled so enthusiastically on the brake-knob, it came off in his hand. He slipped, dropped the knob in our fast-flowing stream and nearly fell in himself. Another neighbour, pushing at the back, stuck his shoulder through a window. Fortunately he didn't hurt himself and as Charles said, what was a pane of glass? The caravan was under cover. That was what really mattered. After a fortnight, we could relax.

Did *he* ever stop to think, I said later that night as we lazed before the sitting-room fire... Saska on my lap, Shebalu on Charles's, Lancelot happily cracking nuts out in the porch... Did he ever stop to think what other people did? Stored

their caravans in their gardens? Under a carport, under a tarpaulin, or even standing in the open? I bet nobody else would have worked so hard to remove all the rubbish we had.

Maybe not, said Charles, but it would be worth it in the long run. That caravan was a little beauty. Think of us going off to Cornwall and Scotland in it. Taking the cats. Maybe even taking Annabel. In the *caravan*? I said incredulously. Charles said he didn't see why not.

Changing the subject, he said (he could see I was about to raise objections to the idea of the caravan doubling as a horse-box)... talking of self-sufficiency... he'd been talking to Tim after we'd got the caravan in. Had I heard about him and the graveyard?

Six

It dated from the days when this was a mining area. In the late 1700s, at the time of the Industrial Revolution, there was a tremendous demand for calamine, which was used with copper to make brass. Our hills contained particularly good calamine – the finest, some said, in Europe – and miners came into the district from Wales, Cornwall, Yorkshire, building their own cottages in the Valley by the stream, or straggling higgledy-piggledy up the hill.

By the 1890s the calamine had run out, however, and the miners moved away. To Australia. To the Klondyke. A few of the less adventurous became farm labourers. Eventually most of the cottages fell into decay, helped on by the local Squire on whose great-grandfather's land the miners had squatted in the first place and who now, when a cottage became empty, took the roof off and left the walls to crumble so that the land could revert to his pheasants.

When we came to the Valley there were only four cottages still standing in it, though there were more at the top of the hill. Up there, too, was a heap of stones which according to tradition had once been the miners' chapel and adjoining it a bramble patch surrounded by a crumbling wall – a small enclosure, about thirty feet by forty. It was said to have been the chapel graveyard, though nobody was really sure about it.

Prior to our coming the estate had been broken up and the chapel ruins sold as a site for a bungalow. The enclosure, however, had been excluded from the sale and left sleeping beneath its brambles, and thus it stayed until a stone fell off the wall and Miss Wellington started to worry.

Miss Wellington was always worrying. Everlastingly, monumentally, and with disaster as her lodestar at the end of it. When it snowed, for instance, she worried about people getting their cars up out of the Valley. When the cars were all up and parked safely at the farm, from where the track out to the main road was usually easy, Miss Wellington would immediately start worrying about the hill being cleared so that the cars (though she didn't own one) could get down again. When we first had Annabel she worried about her being lonely and pleaded with us to let her have a foal. On the two occasions when Annabel was thought to be *enceinte* (actually she was having everybody on) Miss Wellington immediately started panicking in circles in case anything should go wrong. When the stone fell off the graveyard wall, needless to say, it afforded endless permutations for worrying.

The whole thing might fall on somebody, she said. Father Adams pointed out that as it was only three feet high they'd

have to be lying down before it could. 'Unless 'twas old Fred comin' home from the Rose and Crown,' he added. 'I've seen he afore now on his hands and knees.' It was a joke of course, but Miss Wellington didn't take it that way. The wall *was* on Fred's route home from the Rose and Crown. From that time on, when he was going past at closing time – needless to say on his feet – he was apt to have a torch shone on him from Miss Wellington's gateway while she waited for him or the wall to fall down.

Came the spring and she thought up another worry. There could be adders in there, she said. So there could. This is adder country and nobody underestimates the possibilities. But it wasn't likely, as she colourfully imagined, that while the three-foot wall had contained them like a snake-pit (conveniently overlooking the broken gate which had stood ajar for years) the moment one stone was off they'd come leaping over in their hordes, attacking people in all directions. Particularly Fred Ferry, one gathered, coming past on hands and knees.

She complained to the Parish Council. So did everybody else. They'd had enough of Miss Wellington and the wall. The Council lobbed back a speedy statement explaining why they couldn't replace the stone. If they did, they said, they'd be accepting responsibility and if any more stones fell off, they'd be liable if anybody got hurt and the cost would go on the rates.

They would, they added placatingly, try to find out whose responsibility it *was*. Father Adams said we could write that lot off then. He'd heard that one before. They'd send somebody a letter, wait for a reply, chew it over at a meeting six months later... 'Took 'em two years once to get a seat

on the green,' he reminisced. "N then they put 'n up back to front. Cemented 'n so people sat with their legs stickin' uphill. Took another two years to get 'n turned round.'

How right he was. The following winter, with letters to the Rector, the Church Commissioners and the local Methodist headquarters behind them, the Council wrote a final abortive missive to some obscure sect in Wales, announced that they had now explored every avenue – and, following a frost, two more stones fell off.

Miss Wellington nearly had a fit. She envisaged the wall coming down like an avalanche – all three feet high of it, with Fred Ferry underneath, needless to say. She envisaged it alternatively happening in a snowstorm and cars running into it, with bodies strewn Excelsior-like on the ice. To try to placate her somebody replaced the stones (anonymously, not to incur responsibility) – and then, suddenly seeing it as a solution to his problems, not the least of which was that he was Miss Wellington's neighbour, Tim Bannett suggested that he should clear the graveyard and use it as an extension to his garden.

The Parish Council gave their approval as being a way of getting it looked after – carefully pointing out, of course, that permission wasn't really theirs to give. Miss Wellington was delighted. Tim and Liz were her two ewe lambs. The rest of the village was equally happy that somebody else had taken on the job – for nothing, moreover – which only went to show how stupid people could be. Until it suddenly dawned on them that Tim had got some land for nothing.

He hadn't really. He wasn't laying claim to the graveyard. He was only going to use it as an allotment in return for keeping it in order. But he'd got the use of it and they hadn't.

They'd let *land* slip through their fingers. From under their very noses – and to a comparative newcomer, too. Half the village promptly said 'twas sacrilege and he shouldn't be allowed to use it. The other half claimed that by rights it ought to be theirs. Their forefathers had lived next door, or had owned land opposite or adjoining. Fred Ferry said his granddad used to graze sheep in there.

How that made it his by rights, or was more respectful than growing vegetables in it, derived from logic clear only to Fred. On one thing he and the rest of the village were united, however. They wouldn't, they told each other at every opportunity, fancy eating anything grown in *there*.

Tim, presumably with thoughts in that direction himself, ordered several loads of topsoil. To keep everybody happy he decided also to avoid the corner where there were mounds. In fact there were only two, the rest of the ground had obviously never been turned, but in a village you never can win.

He did everything he could. Rather than have the topsoil tipped in soullessly from a lorry he had it piled in his driveway and wheeled it reverently across by wheelbarrow. When he was over there working he always took off his hat. In order that people could see where the mounds were and appreciate that he was respecting them he heaped them even higher and planted daffodils on top. All he got for his trouble was that when strangers spotted the unmistakable outlines and stopped to consider the matter over the wall, there was always somebody on hand, strategically placed so the Bannetts could hear them, to expound the ethics of the affair. That young folk nowadays had no sense of what was decent and proper; that if the truth were known the plot

really belonged to them; that they wouldn't fancy eatin' any of they cabbages... and to speculate what, by current values, the graveyard was worth as land.

The other thing that occupied the village that winter was working out why we'd bought a caravan. That we were going to sell the cottage and travel abroad was one of the rumours that came back to us. That we were going to start a caravan park was another. Even the closest of our local acquaintances – Tim, Father Adams and Fred Ferry, who knew we'd bought it so we could get away in it when the fancy took us and, we hoped, take the cats – had their own opinion as to how the venture would work out. The caravan might have come down the hill all right, they informed us regularly. They'd bet us anything we liked we'd never get it *up*.

That, however, was a problem for the future. Meantime we had a more immediate one with Sass. Following an unfortunate oversight on my part he'd reverted to his neurosis about wool. Not just chewing holes in it, as many Siamese do (cat psychologists say it's because they're lonely), but treating it with hostility; not in any circumstances to be slept on; and if he got the chance he used it as a lavatory.

It stemmed from the evening we brought him home as a kitten and introduced him to Shebalu. We put him in a cage-fronted basket, thinking he'd feel safer speaking to her from in there. Unfortunately instead of approaching him with caution, as Seeley had done to her when she was a kitten (adult cats are normally more afraid of strange kittens than the kittens are of them) Shebalu had put her nose to the bars, sworn horrible oaths and threatened to eat him, and Sass, unable to escape, had had diarrhoea on his blanket.

It was that, I felt sure, which had given him his thing about wool. It was obvious from the first that he was a cat who thought and you could practically see what he was thinking. In this new house you used wool as a lavatory – wasn't that what had been there when he'd had the accident in his basket? Furthermore he'd better continue to use it if he wanted to propitiate the cat-gods. Wasn't that the obvious reason why he'd survived such a ferocious attack by the Enemy?

Obviously fearing further attack, Sass wetted everything woollen he could find in the days that followed. The fresh blanket I gave him that night. The nest of sweaters I put for him on our bed. He'd have wetted a sweater with Charles inside it one night – Charles happened to be quietly snoozing – if I hadn't spotted the look on his face and whipped him away before he could do it.

Long after Shebalu had accepted him and he slept in her arms at night as if he were her own, his phobia about wool remained. Give them a hot water bottle wrapped in a towel and they lay against it like Botticelli angels. Put it in a woollen cover or wrap it in a sweater and Sass worked like a beaver all night. Next morning, inevitably wetted, that being part of the ritual, sweater and bottle would lie discarded on the floor and Sass would be regarding us with the air of Sir Galahad after a vigil. He'd kept off the bogeyman but Only Just said his earnest, round-eyed expression. Shebalu, having had to sleep bottleless all night, would be watching us direly from another chair. It was all her fault, we told her. Scaring him the way she had. We'd never had this trouble with any other kitten.

Eventually, by keeping wool away from him, we cured him of his fetish about wetting. When there wasn't anything

woollen around he used his box with an untroubled mind. There was just one rug in the sitting-room which apparently was some sort of touchstone and which we had to cover with a rubber sheet – weighing it down with two earthboxes and an array of ornaments otherwise Sass would lift it up and perform religiously underneath.

Other than that we'd got him out of it. We even got him round to sleeping on a blanket – with a hot water bottle under it moreover, which with Sass was really something. And then I made my unfortunate mistake. Shut him in our bedroom without an earthbox – with a nest of sweaters and a hot water bottle on the bed.

It was the result of all the double-checking we'd got the habit of over the years. To lock wardrobes, for instance, to keep our blue-eyed demons out, and then go back and have another look to see we hadn't locked them inside instead. To turn off the electricity at the mains before we went out in the car (Solomon used to poke at wires and switches)... and then, halfway up the hill, reverse speedily back again, unable to remember whether we'd done it or not. In this case I'd gone up to check that the hot water bottle wasn't leaking. It had dripped a little when I screwed it up and if it did that on the sweaters, Sass might get ideas...

That thought was actually in my *mind*, so how, having checked the bottle and patted their heads, I could have absentmindedly closed the bedroom door on them, leaving them with innocent expressions, cut off completely from their earthboxes...

I knew there was something wrong when we came back two hours later and there were no faces at the hall window to greet us. Even more so when I opened the hall door

and nobody came through it as if shot from a catapult. Kidnapped. Dead. The wardrobe had fallen on them. The usual Siamese owner's thoughts flashed through my mind. Then I looked up the stairs, saw the closed door at the top, heard the sound of rampaging elephants inside... My thoughts switched immediately to those sweaters on the bed. I knew what I was going to find.

He'd done an absolutely outsize wet – through the sweaters, through the quilt, right down to the blankets. The hot water bottle had been dumped on the floor. In a futile hope I picked it up and checked it. Alas, it wasn't the bottle that had done the leaking, though the swamp on the bed was big enough. I looked at the undoubted culprit, watching me warily from the dressing table.

Why couldn't he have used a *corner* in an emergency, like any other cat? I wailed. If it came to that, why couldn't he have held *on* for a mere two hours? Normal cats don't use their boxes every five minutes like demented fountains. Why did *he* have to make such a point of it?

He regarded me with his Elizabethan philosopher look. His face always seemed much longer when he was solemn. I knew how he got Nervous, he said. How did *he* know it would only be two hours? He'd thought it was through not doing it that he and Shebalu had got locked in. He'd only been making a Libation.

He'd done that all right. I had to change all the blankets and it took days, after I'd washed it, to air the quilt. Even then I had to mount guard on it when Sass was anywhere near. He kept sniffing it with an air of unfinished business. More than that, he'd gone right back to his obsession about wool – obviously wetting the sweaters had brought it back

to him. It became his main preoccupation and for a while it felt like ours as well.

Seven

Charles, given to reading peacefully in his armchair after supper, got fed up with seeing Sass eternally going past with one of his socks. He'd take it away, sit on it, resume his reading... The next thing to catch his eye would be Sass going past with the other sock, en route to dumping it by the kitchen door which was the nearest he could get to putting it outside. If it wasn't a sock then it would be one of Charles's sweaters, dragged along as if Sass's very continuance in this world depended on it.

According to him it did. Hadn't he stopped wetting on wool because we'd persuaded him, and got shut in the bedroom as a result? Where he and Shebalu might have been locked for Ever if he hadn't done some conciliatory work on the sweaters? Got to wet this one Too, he would inform us, struggling across the floor with his burden – and Charles would yell, slap his book down exasperatedly, and

make a hurried grab for that. Why did that cat always take *his* sweaters and socks? he demanded. Why couldn't he occasionally take mine?

Because I didn't leave them where Sass could find them. On the bed or the bathroom stool was Charles's usual wont. One day, however, Sass went upstairs. I could hear him thumping around. It sounded as if he was moving a piano, but Siamese activities usually do. When he reappeared he was stumbling along with something big and dark, legs straddled as if he were carrying a pheasant. Charles's sweater, I thought, cocking a glance across the room from where I was watching television – and then I realised it was mine. My new Shetland sweater that I hadn't even worn. It had been on a shelf in the bedroom cupboard.

Charles, it transpired, had put all his things away for once and Sass, searching for a sacrificial offering, must have got the cupboard door open attracted by the peaty scent of the wool, which to him was probably worse even than the ordinary kind. This one smelled Awful, he informed me as he passed. Boy, were we lucky he'd found it. He'd just put it over by the kitchen door and perform his Magic Action on it...

Oh no he wouldn't, I said. I took it away from him and put it behind me in the chair, not wishing to miss the programme I was watching. Next thing I knew, he'd bitten me hard in the arm and I nearly hit the ceiling.

As I say, it needs psychology to understand Siamese cats. He hadn't bitten me because he was angry with me. It was just that I was wearing a woollen cardigan, I had the Shetland sweater behind me, the smell he so disliked was coming from my direction. Ergo, the thing to do was to

seize me by my woollen-clad arm, drag me to the door and wet on *me*.

That, at least, was our interpretation of how his small mind worked about wool. With patience we could probably get him out of it, we thought. What we hadn't bargained for was Shebalu joining in the wetting game – for an entirely different reason.

There was a strange tabby cat coming into our garden. She kept seeing it through the window and getting annoyed. Sass would flatten his ears round the curtain at it, pretend he was a tiger in ambush, leave off next moment to come and see what I was cooking... Not so Shebalu, who would yatter at the intruder like a machine-gun then make straight for the earthbox in the corner.

We'd never had an earthbox in the living-room before. It had been installed as a mental prop for Sass. Now Shebalu would get into it, squat in girl-cat position, nattering away about Not Knowing what things were Coming To. As she talked, indignation would overcome her and she rose higher and higher in the box. As she did, the stream rose with her and inexorably hit the wall. Some people think that she-cats can't spray. They should have seen our Siamese hose.

We dealt with the problem as best we could by tacking polythene sheeting against the wall. (We couldn't remove the box on account of Sass.) When we saw her rear begin to rise we gently sat her down, telling her that girls weren't supposed to do that. Eventually it dawned on us what was upsetting her. She thought the other cat was her rival for Sass.

We were across in the orchard with the pair of them one day when the stranger happened along. We'd learned in the

meantime that her name was Belle and she lived at the top of the hill. Seeing our two she came running through the grass towards them, obviously wanting to play. Sass looked interested. Shebalu growled and crouched. Belle turned tail and fled. Shebalu tried to chase her, but we had her on her lead, so instead she turned on Sass. In an instant she had him down and was kicking the daylights out of him. She'd seen him looking at That Hussy! she yelled. He'd been Encouraging her. No wonder she kept coming into Our Garden. She bet he'd sleep on *her* stomach if he could.

We didn't realise it was jealousy at first. We separated them and carried them back to the cottage wondering what on earth had come over her. We put Sass down in the sitting-room, all round eyes and ruffled fur, and hovered ready to grab him if she sprang again. Instead she marched into the earthbox and sprayed heartily against the wall – not even bothering to sit first, she was so furious. She then came out, having relieved her feelings and sniffed at Sass, who was regarding her as if she were a Gorgon. Suppose she'd better clean him up, she said, and forthwith proceeded to do it.

We'd have thought it was a momentary aberration – maybe she'd mistaken him in her anger for the other cat – but for the fact that from that time on she only had to catch the merest whiff of Belle, and she immediately pitched into Sass.

Once I had to carry her down from the hillside behind the cottage completely beside herself with rage. Smelling Belle's scent on a gorse bush – seeing, which was worse, Sass interestedly sniffing at it – she'd leapt upon him with the fury of a Parisian Apache dancer. I separated them. She rushed at him again and I picked him up. She'd Kill Him

when I put him down, she informed him. Sass, who always goes completely silent in moments of stress, dug his claws into my shoulder and prepared for take-off. I couldn't manage them both, so I let him go and grabbed Shebalu instead. She is half his size and easier to handle. Holding her firmly by her back legs and the scruff of her neck, I ran back along the hillside shouting for Charles.

'What is it? An adder?' he demanded, rushing out of the kitchen door clutching the poker. Fred Ferry was as usual out in the lane.

'It's Sass!' I shouted. 'Shebalu's attacked him and he's bleeding. I've brought her back to keep them apart, but I've had to leave him behind!'

Charles started to run. I knew what he was thinking. Since we'd lost Seeley we'd never left a cat out of doors alone, and now Sass was loose somewhere – on a trailing lead, which was dangerous in itself – and goodness knew what he might meet up with.

'How far back did you leave him?' he asked, hurriedly unfastening the gate.

'Don't know what thee two bist panicking about,' said Fred laconically. 'There he is coming along behind thee.'

Sure enough, following Shebalu and me at a distance, was a woebegone little figure. Frightened, left behind, maybe thinking I didn't want him – still his one thought was to stay close. Never, of all the Siamese who have given their hearts to us, has one loved us quite so devotedly as Sass.

Which was all very well but he had a piece out of one ear and Shebalu had hit him on his nose, which was bleeding. What did she mean by it? I asked her. Her? said Shebalu, calm as a Quaker now they were indoors. It was all *his* fault

for encouraging that other cat. She strolled across, looked him over and licked his fur back into place. He was as good as new now, she informed us.

He wouldn't have been for long, the way she was beating him up, but in March we had a week of heavy snow. It kept Belle away. Our two rarely went out. When they did, it was up a solid, snow-packed track from which her scent had been obliterated. Shebalu forgot about her and Sass could breathe again – which was more than could be said for the rest of us.

Miss Wellington was on the trail. The weather forecast had given snow – heavy over Western hills, which was us. This explained why our starlings had arrived the previous day, several weeks earlier than usual. They nested in our roof every year – they had entrances under the tiles above the gutter – and they moved in like a migrating tribe of Red Indians. We could hear them up there, scuffling in one corner, banging away in another, protesting as they squeezed narrowly in through the holes. Making more noise than any of the others, as he had done for several years previously, was one we could distinguish because he'd somewhere or other learned to wolf-whistle.

'If theest stopped up they holes,' Father Adams told us every spring, 'they 'ouldn't get in there tearing up thee roof.'

Actually we wouldn't have turned them out for anything. It had been their nesting place for years. But one or two of them did bang away as if they were using steam-hammers. They'd start up at dawn and I'd lie in bed listening, wondering what on earth they were up to. Extending their quarters? They certainly couldn't be catching insects at that

speed, unless the beams were riddled with woodworm... I'd wake Charles to listen. He'd say if it was that rotten the starlings wouldn't make much difference and turn over and go back to sleep. I'd go on listening. Every now and then there'd be a piercing Whee-eeew, as if somebody was saying Now you've done it...

That, however, was normal breeding-season behaviour. It was different the day before the snow. The starlings came in, rustled about a bit, as if they were unpacking their bags. There were a few flutters and scuffles and squawks. We heard the familiar wolf-whistle, probably saying Gosh, fancy finding this place still standing. Then they settled down, as if they were waiting for something – and twenty-four hours later we had the snow.

It came during the night. Everybody in the Valley slept peacefully, knowing that the cars were all up at the farm. We'd all heard the forecast and Miss Wellington had phoned everybody anyway, and had stood at her gate to check the cars as they went up one by one. At seven next morning the phone rang again.

'It *can't* be her,' I said. It was, though. Ringing all of us in turn to tell us the village was cut off. There was a drift beyond the farm, right down to the main road – she'd already been out to have a look at it. She was terribly worried, she said. Nobody could get to work. Shouldn't we get up early and try to dig through?

In her mind's eye she obviously saw us all digging away as in the salt mines. Out to the main road by nine o'clock and those who worked in town, at their desks by ten. A combination of 'Business as Usual', 'The Mail must go Through' and 'Valiant Expedition to the Arctic'. What she

was overlooking was that it was a good half-mile out to the main road and the drift was packed as high as the hedge-tops. Even with elephants we couldn't have got through that lot. There was nothing for it but to wait for the snow-plough.

There being more important roads than ours we had to wait for several days, though Miss Wellington rang the Council every morning as if we were Mafeking. Meanwhile, cut off, unable to get away, the rest of the village turned its mind to other pursuits. Men sawed wood. Women baked bread because the baker couldn't get through. Children appeared with sledges. People helped one another to clear their paths. Miss Wellington, a woollen scarf over her hat and wearing enormous boots, helped everybody busily. When Charles and I went up to try to get to the village shop for milk, she was scraping away frantically in the drive of the house on the corner. When we came back an hour later, having navigated drifts that had piled up like ice caverns and frozen wastes that looked like the Antarctic, Miss Wellington was scraping away outside the Rose and Crown, obviously trying to set an example.

'Worried about thee pint?' Fred Ferry jovially enquired, stamping his feet as he went through the door. Miss Wellington regarded him frostily. He wouldn't joke if he needed an ambulance, she said, obviously still harbouring visions of him under the graveyard wall. And how was the milkman going to get through? And the man who came for the insurance?

They didn't. For days we clambered over the drifts for the milk. Somebody always brought Miss Wellington's. The insurance man, who covered several villages on a bicycle, got so behind he didn't come for weeks.

Miss Wellington continued to worry, however – if it wasn't about our being cut off by the snow, it was whether the stream would flood when the thaw came. Occasionally, by way of a change, she would potter across to the graveyard and do a stint of worrying about that. Was Tim *sure* the wall was safe? She was so concerned about Mr Ferry. That poor curly kale, weighed down by all that snow – wouldn't it be better for it if Tim cleared it off? Those dear, dear daffodils, flowering so bravely under their covering – she wished somebody would go to their rescue...

He wished somebody'd rescue *him*, Tim remarked one day, somewhat at the end of his tether. 'Ah!' replied Miss Wellington. 'We shouldn't wait for rescue! We should go out and do things for ourselves!'

So help him, said Tim, before he knew where he was she had him round the corner digging out that drift. She never gave up, did she? He could see her waving the troops up the Heights of Abraham.

Her name was Wellington, not Wolfe, but he had something there. Miss Wellington never gave in. Fred Ferry said there were times when he thought this Bannett bloke almost deserved the graveyard, living next door to she.

Eight

Sass liked the snow once he decided it was safe, but it took several excursions for him to be sure of it. After every fall he would venture cautiously out and try the surface with a paw. It would crumble. He'd reach out a little further and put his weight on it. Being a big lad, his paw would sink through. He'd reach out as far as he could with the other. Darned if it didn't look as if he was doing the crawl, said Father Adams. What was he going to think up next?

A good many things. Sass found the snow exciting. Even when he got used to it he still went at it as if he were swimming. While Shebalu stuck to the path when we took them out, shaking her paws in protest at every step, he would dash into any drift he could find like a valiantly paddling retriever. Back indoors, invigorated, he'd look round for something to do – which was how he came to

institute his marathon round the settee, which even for a Siamese was pretty peculiar.

I'd seen Shebalu doing it once or twice. Our room is wide and L-shaped. She'd hurry across from under the table, round the settee, back across the room and under the table... never running, just walking quietly but hurriedly, like the White Rabbit in *Alice in Wonderland*.

We decided she was doing it for exercise. Being indoors so much in winter she probably thought her legs needed stretching. Two or three circuits were enough for her, however, then she'd curl up in a chair and go to sleep. Not so Sass who, when he took up the idea, circled settee and table like a merry-go-round.

Once, while I counted, he went round twenty-six times non-stop. Charles said he was probably jogging. It wasn't as simple as that, I said. I reckoned it had become another of his compulsions.

It certainly had. We had a performance every evening. Round and round and round. It went beyond exercise, beyond merely copying Shebalu – you could tell it by his expression. If he *didn't* go round and round like that, Something Terrible would happen.

That was bad enough. Eventually it even affected Charles, who said there ought to be an Outward Bound course for cats. He knew one cat who'd be on it like a rocket, he said, before he had us all going round in circles. But Sass then developed another compulsion and worked the two of them together.

It involved going up the bookcase and it was also started by Shebalu, of whom I was beginning to have my suspicions. She knew Sass wasn't a good climber. She knew he had

this thing about having to copy her. So every single night without fail she would leap to the top shelf of the bookcase and sit looking down at him expectantly for his reaction, which was to erupt from chair or hearthrug as if she'd pressed a button and start worrying about getting up there himself.

Another cat would have ignored the challenge. Pretended it didn't matter. In similar circumstances Solomon used to go off and climb something simpler to satisfy honour – usually Charles's dressing-gown behind the bedroom door, which was known as Solomon's ladder. Not so Sass. From the expression on his face, if he didn't make it up the bookcase the haunts would get him. So I'd help him up. I couldn't win, of course. He'd then sit there and worry about coming down again – silently, as is usual when Sass is in a crisis, but you couldn't fail to know he was up there doing it. For one thing there was Shebalu, now back on the hearthrug herself, looking up interestedly as if he was about to jump from a skyscraper. For another, every now and again he'd put a paw on the top of the standard lamp and peer anxiously down through the shade. 'Not through there!' I'd yell and rush to stand on a chair so that he could get down via my shoulder...

Once a night was enough for the bookcase routine but within minutes of completing that he'd remember the other thing that kept off the haunts and he'd be off on his trek round the settee. If he saw us watching him he stopped and lurked, but the moment we looked away, on he went, round and round, as if he was on a treadmill. The only guaranteed way to break the sequence was to open the door

to the kitchen, through which he'd vanish quietly on his next trip round to see if there was anything to eat.

Did I think he was mental? Charles sometimes asked. Not from the way he nipped into the kitchen, I said.

It was odd, all the same. He did other odd things, too, though they didn't impinge quite so much on our nerves. The business of moving pens and pencils and paintbrushes around, for instance, took place after we'd gone to bed. At first it was just an odd pencil which I'd find lying tooth-marked on the rug in the morning. I'd pick it up and put it back in the vase on the Welsh dresser, commenting that Sass was being a retriever again.

Charles, whose hobby is painting, keeps his brushes and pencils in that vase, on hand for the moment of inspiration. He didn't mind Sass taking one pencil – in fact he regarded the tooth marks with affection. Strong little teeth. He certainly gripped things tightly. Funny little chap, wasn't he? he said.

He didn't say that when, as was inevitable with Sass, there was a build-up in the operation. When we began to come down in the morning to find brushes and pencils strewn around as if our dark man had been distributing largesse. They were scattered across the carpet. They were poked under rugs and cushions. Some of them we didn't find for days. He began to hide my pens, too, which I have a habit of leaving on a shelf of the bookcase. Sometimes I couldn't find a thing to write with.

It had become another of his compulsions. One which occupied a lot of time. He took to sitting on the Welsh dresser when he thought it was our bedtime, willing us to go upstairs so he could start. As if he were waiting for

the coast to be clear before he started running the brandy barrels, said Charles. Perhaps he'd been a smuggler in a previous incarnation.

Charles was still reasonably light-hearted about it when he made that remark, though he was getting a bit concerned about his chewed-up brush handles. Pencils he didn't mind so much but paint-brushes were expensive, he said. What was more, it wasn't hygienic.

Rather more hygienic than Sass's next development, which was to start putting the brushes in his earthbox. At that point the project came to a sudden end in a strong smell of Dettol and references to one-way tickets to Siam. The vase joined the onion sack upstairs in the *verboten* room and Sass was most upset, though he showed no sign of it during the day. Only after we went to bed that night did our dark man, normally so silent, start howling... great, soulful howls that announced he'd been doing his Best. He hoped *he* wouldn't be blamed for falling down on the brush ritual. He'd have gone on moving them for Ever and Ever. If anybody's whiskers were going to fall out, it ought to be that Rotten Old Charles's.

Hating to hear him howling so disconsolately – besides which he kept us awake – we compromised by leaving a selection of removables on the dresser. Pencils he'd already chewed. Old pens that needed refills. A broken wooden curtain ring that Sass immediately adopted as his favourite talisman. His other treasures were moved only during the night, but his ring appeared constantly during the day. Hooked from under the piano. Tossed in front of us to beguile us into playing with him. From time to time, when he thought it necessary, laid reverently in his earthbox.

There were times, particularly when he was carrying it round the settee, when he looked like a South Sea Islander with a nose-ring doing a war dance. What did it matter, however, so long as it kept him happy and we were the only ones who knew about it? Letting anyone else see him was a different matter. It would have been added evidence of our oddness. Meantime the thaw came and spring arrived, heralded by Annabel getting a dose of colic.

It would have been understandable if it had happened while we were snow-bound and she couldn't go into her field – when she spent the day alternately eating hay in her stable and looking out over her tiny half-door. Charles had made it specially to fit her height, so she could get her head over the top. Even so she kept bawling about how bored she was and that she wanted to go out. So every day we took her for a walk up the hill, where a track had been trodden in the snow.

Annabel loved it. The people who lived at the top gave her sweets and fondled her ears. She had her photograph taken standing importantly by a snowman. Always one for effect, this was when she behaved at her best, with a daily captive audience. She plodded along behind me being Annabel Going To The Klondike, walking obediently in my tracks. She made no attempt now, as was her usual practice on walks, to nip my bottom and then mockingly shake her head, her mouth wide open in a disparaging donkey laugh which held all the more meaning for being silent.

One afternoon, encouraged by Miss Wellington, we tried to take her out on to the main road. She was sure it was possible and it would set such a good example, she said, if our dear little donkey could do it.

We tried, not by way of an example, but to see how far we could go over the drift. We might have got through – it had packed like ice on top and Annabel is as sure-footed as a mountain goat – but the wind had come up, loose snow was blowing sideways off the fields, and we walked into a veritable blizzard. Without altering pace for an instant our four-footed friend turned round and started back. Annabel believes in looking after Annabel – no setting examples for her. We emerged like a set piece sculptured in ice, white from head to foot. People said it looked most spectacular and photographed that little incident too. We often wondered what they captioned it in their albums. 'Pioneers en route for the Yukon', or 'The queer lot who live in the Valley?'

They'd certainly have thought us queer if they'd seen us when Annabel had colic, but fortunately that took place in the dark.

It was the day after it started to thaw. As I say, it would have been understandable had it happened during the snow, when she mostly stood in her stable eating and shouting complaints and got very little exercise. But the snow was clearing fast. We'd been able to put her on the hillside behind the cottage, where her donkey paths had turned to slush and the grass was showing through.

Whether she got a chill, whether she ate grass with ice in it, whether Miss Wellington paid her a surreptitious visit and fed her with too many apples – the fact was that when Charles put her in her stable for the night and tipped her bag of bread and carrots into her bowl (we carry the bag ahead of her, rustling it to coax her to follow, otherwise she is likely to disappear deliberately in the wrong direction), instead of tucking into it she stood there with her head

down, sighing and looking mournful. Urged by Charles to eat, she buckled at the knees, lay down and closed her eyes. Then she began to roll and kick her legs and Charles came running for me. It takes two to deal with Annabel when she has colic.

A horse or donkey, rolling in pain, can twist its intestines and die. You have to get them on their feet as fast as possible. Annabel may look small but she is apparently made of cast iron. It was like trying to lift a tank. When we got her up she sagged at the knees and immediately tried to go down again. We half carried her out to the lane, where we put her bridle on her and forced her to walk up and down. It is the recognised treatment for colic, but doing it by torchlight, in a lane deep with slush and with the rain beating down, it looked more as if we were slave-driving some helpless little donkey than doing our best to revive her. We must have looked absolute rotters.

After one car had passed us with slow deliberation, its occupants giving us dirty looks, we took her in on the cottage lawn for privacy. There, in familiar surroundings, she refused to walk at all. She lay on her side and closed her eyes, obviously resigned to leaving the world. At this stage we realised that our outside light was on and we were now more noticeable than ever. Spotlit, she lay there in the pouring rain with Charles and me trying frantically to heave her up. 'Whass be doin' now?' enquired a voice from the darkness. 'Thee dussn't half get up to some capers.'

It was Father Adams. He'd seen our torch light bobbing about in the lane and had come up to see what it was. He helped us lift Annabel, helped rub her down with sacks, helped massage her rotund white stomach. There have

been many occasions when we've been grateful for Father Adams's inquisitiveness and this was definitely one of them. 'Why dussn't try her with a peppermint?' he said at length. ''Tis what the Missis always gives I.'

It hadn't occurred to us. We hadn't any peppermints anyway, but I did have a bottle of peppermint essence. Fervently hoping I was doing the right thing, I poured some on some bread and offered it to her. Whether it actually did the trick... whether she was feeling better anyway... she turned wanly away, turned back again as she caught the smell... Annabel is fond of peppermints. She took the bread, chewing it languidly, with none of her usual gusto, but so long as she could eat at all, you could bet that Annabel was going to live. She ate another piece. We took her into the lane again and marched her up and down the hill by torchlight. This time there was no faltering. We went up and down for quite a while on the advice of Father Adams – to make sure, as he put it, that her guts was properly unknotted. We must have looked even scattier, walking up and down the hill by torchlight, leading a donkey with nothing wrong with her, apparently just for the fun of it. Not that it really worried us. The main thing was, Annabel was all right.

We put her back in her stable. She started on her hay at once and we went down to the cottage to change our soaking clothes. Sass and Shebalu, curled together in the armchair, opened one eye each as we went in. Where had we been? asked Shebalu's expression. *Out* on a night like This? Was it time for supper? queried Sass's lifted nose. Was I going to get their hot milk?

It was far too early. Only half-past seven. Charles commented on how contented they looked. *They* didn't

overeat and get colic, he said with feeling. And if they did, *their* gut wouldn't get twisted. *They* wouldn't lie on the lawn like stranded whales while we got soaked to the perishing skin...

No. They had more subtle methods of getting our attention. Even as he spoke Shebalu got up, yawned, and leapt lightly to the top of the bookcase. Sass, on cue, sat up himself and immediately started looking worried.

Charles groaned, then brightened. Spring was on the way, he said. We'd soon be getting the caravan on the road. Before that, I reminded him, we had a cat house to put up... Charles groaned even louder.

Nine

The cat house was part of our security plan. The remembrance of Seeley's disappearance was always with us and, to guard against the same thing happening again, either Charles or I was always with Sass and Shebalu when they were out and it took up a great deal of time.

We ought to have a house and run for them, I kept saying. They could be out in it in good weather, enjoying the sunshine, while we got on with other things. We'd still accompany them on walks, of course, and watch over them while they hunted, but we wouldn't be continually panicking in between because they'd managed to vanish in a row of cabbages.

Charles, agreeing, said he'd put up a cat house himself. It would only take a couple of weeks. The question was, two weeks from when? He already had three major jobs on hand on which he spent an hour or so in turn when the

spirit moved him. That way, according to him, they got done before one realised it. One day there they were – finished.

The conservatory wasn't for a start. He'd been renovating that for years. People sometimes asked, seeing him on the ladder, whether he was putting it up or pulling it down. Fencing the field beyond the cottage was another of our projects. We'd bought it as an additional paddock for Annabel. Charles had so far put one side fence up really expertly, but it wasn't much use without the others. Thirdly – the item which had top priority at the moment – he was building a dresser in the kitchen.

That, I must admit, was entirely my own fault. The previous autumn, when we'd measured the kitchen for the pine dresser I'd fancied when we brought home the sack of onions, it was to discover that a normal-sized dresser was too small and would look silly and one of the big ones would be far too long. In an unguarded moment I'd thought of the old sideboard out in the woodshed, stowed there years before by Charles. I measured it. It fitted the space exactly. If we used that as a base, I said – faced it with pine-cladding, tiled the top, built pine dresser shelves above it – it would look like a super Swedish-style dresser and make some room in the woodshed into the bargain.

Charles, fired with enthusiasm, said he'd enjoy doing that. Wasn't I glad now he'd kept that dresser? The pine-cladding part wouldn't take more than a week. He'd have the whole thing finished by Christmas.

He might have done if it weren't for the fact that Charles is the world's top perfectionist. When, for instance, he found that the sideboard was veneered he insisted on removing all the veneer before he started. Why I couldn't imagine,

since pine-cladding was to go on top of it, but Charles said when *he* did a job he did it properly. Stripped of the veneer, there were cracks to be filled in and rubbed down. Again I couldn't think why, until Charles explained that the finish was now so perfect it would be a pity to pine-clad it at all. He would varnish it instead, to bring out the grain, which would be quicker and he could start on the top part even sooner.

Unfortunately the varnish turned it a peculiar red colour so he reverted to the idea of pine-cladding. He also decided to give it a new back, and new shelves inside. New bottoms to the drawers, too, while he was at it. I didn't want them sticking, did I? he asked when I said but that would take *ages*.

Oh boy, I said, just give me the chance! Thinking I'd be able to store things in the sideboard from the start, as soon as we'd brought it inside I'd agreed to moving the old kitchen cabinet out to the porch to give Charles more room to work in. I now trudged miles a day carrying cups and plates and cutlery, leaving trails of sawdust behind me, while Charles sawed inspiredly away as if he were Sheraton and the cats played games through the empty drawer holes. Never mind about them sticking. Give me just one drawer I could actually *use*, and I'd stand on my head in celebration.

Add a cat house to the list? Not on your nelly. We, I said firmly, were going to buy one. Even so the thought was with me that, even if we bought the house itself – there were plenty of wooden sheds with windows on the market – Charles would still have to build a run around it and we'd have Project Number Four under way. At which point,

while I was wondering whether my nerves would stand it, the Francises decided to close their Siamese boarding cattery at Low Knap.

Probably the best-known Siamese cattery in England – at one time it was said to be unique in Europe – it is nearly thirty years since Dr and Mrs Francis set the standard for modern cat boarding. Individual houses – separated, not in rows; large, individual runs; complete disinfection when a boarder moved out, even down to the blow-lamping of the earthboxes. Infra-red lamps over beds that were deep-sided and private, cushions to sit on in the windows – there were Siamese who'd boarded there for as long as three years while their owners were over-seas.

That in itself was a tribute to the proprietors. Siamese are peculiar creatures. Some catteries refuse to take them at all, saying they are more trouble than any other type of cat. The Francises, knowing this, specialised in the Oriental breeds, boarding only Siamese, Burmese and Havana. It was like visiting a top racing stable to walk past the runs, seeing an aloof-looking aristocrat in each. In some cases there were two or three aristocrats from the same household, lying there like a pride of lions, gazing with disdain at the rest of the world but keeping a hopeful eye open for the Francises.

Now they had retired. Rather than pass the business on and risk their standards not being maintained, they had closed, which was why we'd bought a caravan. Our cats had always boarded there. Sugieh had been mated there. We'd always left them with every confidence. No place, we said, could ever come up to Low Knap. In future we'd have to take the cats on holiday with us.

Not that I looked forward to it. I was already waking in the clear cold light of dawn envisaging trouble with Sass over his earthbox and positive mayhem when it came to the cooking. Always, in the kitchen, I had to watch out for stealthy paws. Sass in particular could materialise from nowhere. How would I manage in a caravan, cooking with two of them present and no handy door through which to dump them?

It is an ill-wind that blows nobody any good, however. The closing of Low Knap might have landed us with the prospect of taking the cats on holiday – I only hoped I was going to survive it – but it also meant that the Francises had some first-class cat houses and runs to dispose of, and we were able to buy one.

We hired a do-it-yourself van to bring the sections up from Dorset. The rumour went round that we'd been seen driving a lorry piled high with hen houses. According to Father Adams they were speculating at the Rose and Crown as to whether we were planning a caravan park in the new field we'd acquired or had been carried away by watching *The Good Life*.

I explained to him that the field was for Annabel and the 'hen houses' comprised a single cat house. Ah well, he said, he weren't goin' to tell 'em. What with the things they reckoned we were up to, and what young Bannett were doin' with the graveyard, it gave he the belly-ache laughing just to listen to 'em.

So the cat house lay in sections on the lawn throughout the winter, covered by a tarpaulin. We wouldn't need it till the spring and Charles was still busy with the dresser. Meanwhile Tim Bannett had bought a field further up

the lane from ours because he was planning to expand in the goat business. Polly was ready for mating, he said, and he thought of getting a second nanny – he'd need more room than he had at the cottage. Couldn't he graze them round the edges of the graveyard? I asked. He could always fence off the mounds. After all there are still villages where they graze sheep actually in the churchyard, following the medieval custom...

There'd probably be a riot if he did, said Tim. He wouldn't like to, anyway. Apart from which, couldn't we imagine what people'd say about the milk? They'd had enough to say about the bright green hens' eggs.

They had indeed. Fred Ferry swore they'd made his eyes twitch, though the rest of the village attributed that to too much cider. 'Twas St Vitus Dance of the eyeballs,' according to Father Adams, 'and thee dussn't get that through eatin' eggs.'

Anyway, Tim bought the field and kept going to and fro with fencing poles. On his way he usually stopped for a natter with us over the wall, which naturally didn't go unnoticed. Charles, meanwhile, inspired by the first faint stirring of spring took the tarpaulin off the cat house sections and ordered a ton and a half of paving stones for the base on which it was to stand. These, when they came, were dumped outside our gate, the driver saying it was past his knocking-off time.

All of which incidents were pieced together, country-style, into the usual wildly wrong conclusion. We'd bought a field. Tim had bought a field. We were going into partnership together. Caravans in our field, chalets in his – we had the sections all ready on our front lawn. He'd

been seen in his field hammering in posts to mark the sites. There was the paving for the paths outside our gate. We were going to open at Easter. The bookings were rolling in. We were expecting to make our fortunes.

Nobody really believed it, of course. It was just a piece of typical village invention, with somebody adding a bit every time the subject came round like children playing a game at a party. The touch that tickled us most was added by one of our neighbours who went abroad from time to time on business. Vastly proud of the fact, he always made sure that everybody knew without actually telling them directly. The next time the subject was raised in the Rose and Crown – 'Well, I'm off to Bahrain,' he announced, 'I only hope that by the time I get back there won't be wooden huts all over the hillside.'

There wouldn't have been much time for it, since he was only going for three days. As it was, there wasn't even one hut. Apart from the fact that the cat house was going in the garden – on my best flower bed, being the sunniest and most secluded spot – it took us three weeks' solid work to erect it, and even then we were racing against time. Digging up the plants, levelling the ground which sloped considerably – that in itself, took days. Then there was laying the paving-stone foundation for the house – cementing it and waiting for it to set. Meanwhile Charles laid a frame of paving stones on which to stand the run, this being most important. We could fill in the centre at our leisure, Dr Francis had told us, but if we didn't put the framework of the run on paving right from the start, however much our two might languish when we put them in it saying they gave in, we had them Beaten, as soon as our backs were turned they'd

be tunnelling as if they were in Colditz. Siamese cats, he said, can dig like moles.

They are certainly intelligent. As soon as the house was up our two recognised it immediately, marching familiarly through the door and sniffing around. They jumped on the shelf on one side and peered out of the window. He remembered this, said Sass – but why wasn't the Francises' garden outside? He jumped down, crossed the floor and reared up puzzledly beneath the other window. Where, he demanded, was the shelf that used to be Over Here?

We'd omitted that one because, it being such a good-sized house, I fancied working in it myself during the summer. I could see myself in there with my typewriter and the cats, enjoying the drowsy, bee-humming sunshine. Sheltered by the overhanging nut tree, the scent of lilac in the air... but for that there wasn't room for a shelf beneath each of the windows. The second one, in any case, as I lifted up Sass and showed him, would only have looked out on the garage wall. That wouldn't have been interesting now, would it? I said. Apparently it would. Sass kept looking for his missing shelf all the summer.

This is jumping ahead, though. We still had to put up the run and bolt the big wire frames together. Sass shinned up the inside of the first frame the moment he saw it in position – propped up temporarily with poles while we aligned it, minus the other three sides or roof. He looked like a commando tackling an assault course. It was a good eight feet up to the top. This, he said excitedly, was how they used to try Fruitlessly to Escape at Low Knap. Gosh, he exclaimed when he got to the top. What had happened to the roof?

Only he would try to climb out of a run which had only one side and no top to it, which was how another local legend arose – that he was crossed with a monkey, which people often say about Siamese. Actually they had reason for it in his case. He has this prehensile-looking bend in his tail, and when I coaxed him to back down on to my shoulder from his marooned position at the top of the frame, he *would* stand with it hooked round my neck.

At last the house and run were up, however. Two days later a ginger cat was seen inside it. At which the village had no doubt as to what we were up to. We were opening a boarding establishment for cats.

They were wrong again. The cat belonged to my Aunt Louisa, who'd gone to Canada for three weeks. She lived alone now and Ginger was her sole companion. She fed him on minced beef and plaice. When relations invited her to Winnipeg she said she couldn't leave Ginger at a cattery, he liked his minced beef sharp at twelve. On the premise, no doubt correct, that they wouldn't watch the clock for him if he boarded anywhere, she said she couldn't possibly go.

Louisa is my favourite aunt. She helped bring me up. She would walk barefoot to the ends of the earth for me. She *was* to go to Winnipeg, Charles and I told her. We would look after Ginger ourselves. No, he couldn't sleep with us, he'd have to live in the cat house. But it was a cat house fit for a king. And, I promised her earnestly, he should have his minced beef sharp at twelve.

So Louisa flew off. My cousin Dee drove her to Gatwick. Charles and I couldn't go or Ginger would have missed his twelve o'clock feed. And if I muttered things under my

breath for the next three weeks as I frantically minced beef or steamed plaice, that was nothing to the language used by Sass and Shebalu as, four times a day, they watched him eat. I shouldn't have given him four meals a day, of course. Grown cats should only have two. But I'd promised Louisa, and just suppose he wilted... I turned the mincer handle faster at the thought of it.

When they were in the garden for their own look around, oddly enough our two scarcely seemed to notice him. He spent a lot of time sitting in the cat house window and so long as he wasn't actually out in the run... Whether it was because he was a big cat and discretion seemed wiser than valour; whether it was that to our two the cat house represented Low Knap and at Low Knap they'd been used to seeing other boarders... the fact was that they passed the cat house with scarcely a glance on their way up and down the garden.

Indoors it was a vastly different matter. The side window in our bedroom overlooked Ginger's run and for the next three weeks its conveniently broad sill constituted Siamese Intelligence Headquarters.

He could see his Ears! (Sass's own enormous pair would go up like huge black dhow-sails). He was Looking Out! (Shebalu would crouch, flat as a leaf, like a secret service agent on a cliff-top.) He was in the run! (The pair of them, caution forgotten, would press noses to the window to look down.) They spent hours up there watching him. At least it kept them quiet, said Charles. You couldn't say that, though, at meal times. I used to put in Ginger's food dish, give him a pat and nip smartly in and upstairs to watch the reaction.

He'd got Fish for breakfast... Grrrrr, growled Shebalu. Who did we think *he* was, anyway? Giving him fish and she'd only had tinned rabbit. At Low Knap they'd All had The Same. She'd rattle her teeth at him. At lunchtime it would be Sass. That cat down there was eating Minced Beef. Minced *Beef* – and he, Sass the Important, didn't get any lunch at all!

Wails would rend the air. That was when I started giving them a tit-bit at lunchtime – Sass always managed to look so thin. They ate it in triumph in the bedroom windowsill – though it was still, observed Sass looking down, Not As Much As I Gave I Him.

Louisa wrote to say she'd arrived in Winnipeg. We were very relieved to hear that. Dee had seen her on to the plane, relations were to meet her off it – on the face of it there hadn't been much that could go wrong. It was just that we knew from experience that if anybody's luggage did get lost – or if somebody got their foot stuck in the disembarkment gangway or left behind in the loo if the plane stopped off in Iceland... you could bet on it being Louisa. Things always happened to her.

She wrote again. She'd been to Moosejaw. To Calgary. To Banff National Park, where she'd seen a bear. There was a plane strike on in Canada but we weren't to worry. Cousin Len had checked with Wardair. If the return plane couldn't take off from Winnipeg, they were going to take the passengers by bus down to Grand Forks in North Dakota. Whatever happened she would be back on the sixth of June. She hoped Ginger was eating his minced beef.

He was indeed. Bang on the dot of twelve there he was at his dish, watched, like one of those clocks on which figures

appear and do things on the hour, by two incredulous faces from aloft. By the time we got to the sixth of June and Charles and I drove to Gatwick (we had arranged to bring her back) I could honestly say, hand on heart, that he hadn't missed his minced beef by a second. Her plane was due at Gatwick at seven in the morning. We left the cottage at five. She was to wait in the airport lounge, we'd told her by letter... we'd probably be there around eight. We couldn't leave any earlier what with Annabel to put out to pasture, Sass and Shebalu to take for their walk and feed – and of course, come what might, the plaice to be poached for Ginger's breakfast.

We drove via Salisbury Plain and Aldershot. It is a pleasant route and actually a quicker way from the cottage. It takes us an hour to get on to the motorway at Bristol, whereas in that time we can be well across Wiltshire. We stopped for a snack beyond Stonehenge. Gosh, I was tired, I said. I'd been awake all night worrying about having to get up before four – but at least we were on time. If we picked her up at eight, we'd be back before twelve. Ginger wouldn't have missed his minced beef *once*. I'd developed a fetish about that – like Sass and his earthbox, said Charles. Did I think the ruddy cat would turn into a pumpkin?

Did I realise also that Louisa might not *be* on the plane, particularly if she'd had to go to Dakota? Her cousins wouldn't have been allowed to accompany her on the bus. Goodness knew what she might have got up to.

We imagined practically every possibility after that. We saw her losing her ticket, leaving her passport behind, getting locked in the lavatory at Grand Forks. We visualised every possibility in fact, but the one that actually happened.

We got to Gatwick later than we'd intended. There'd been a traffic hold-up in Guildford, miles of road up between there and Dorking... I went haring into the airport. There was nothing on the arrival board. Good-oh, I thought. She hadn't got in yet. We hadn't kept her waiting. I asked the Wardair clerk when their Winnipeg plane was due. She consulted her list. Flight 359 from Winnipeg, she told me, wasn't due till tomorrow morning.

We should have realised it, of course. On the outward flight, travelling with the sun, Louisa *had* arrived the same day. Coming the other way, due to the time-lag, she wouldn't be back until the seventh. It wasn't her fault. She hadn't done the trip before. It was we who should have checked. All of which didn't alter the fact that while we stood there starkly at Gatwick, she was blissfully asleep in Winnipeg.

There was nothing for it, said Charles philosophically. We'd have to go home, see to the animals, then drive up again that night. We dared not risk going to bed. We'd never get up in the morning.

I had a vision of our whizzing up and down past Stonehenge, three times in a single day. We couldn't *do* it, I wailed. I was dead beat already. 'Oh yes we can,' said Charles.

We would have done, too, but for the traffic on the road. It was much heavier than it had been earlier. There were interminable hold-ups at the sections under repair and we realised more and more how tired we were.

'We just can't do it,' I said at length. 'We'd have to start back as soon as we got home. Look. Annabel's on the hillside – she'll be all right. The cats have got plenty of water. For

our own sakes we'd better stay up here for the night. We'll be back to feed them by mid-morning.'

So that was what we did. We stayed at Dorking. We didn't sleep a wink, of course, imagining two Siamese watching for us forlornly out of the window and Ginger fading away without his minced beef. At least we were on the dot at Gatwick next morning, however, when the Winnipeg plane came in. All he hoped, muttered Charles, was that she was actually on it and hadn't brought half of Winnipeg with her...

'She *couldn't*,' I protested.

'Don't you believe it,' said Charles. And for an awful moment I thought she had. When the doors opened and Louisa came through, she was pushing a trolley loaded with suitcases and carrier bags.

All was well. As usual she was helping others – bringing out an elderly couple's luggage as well as her own. We grabbed her and her belongings, hustled her out and into the car, explained that we'd been up there since the previous morning. 'The cats didn't have their supper last night,' I said. 'We're in a hurry to get home.'

I didn't mention that Ginger had also missed his previous day's minced beef and fortunately it didn't occur to Louisa. All the way back to Somerset, while Charles and I drove blearily in turn, she chatted away about what she'd *done*, where'd she'd *been*, how she was looking forward to seeing her cat.

We arrived at the cottage. Walked down the path. Thank goodness there were two Siamese faces at the window. Distinctly indignant but at least they were there, and Annabel was bawling up on the hill. There was – even more

thank goodness – a ginger cat sitting bolt upright in the cat-run, obviously none the worse for his fast.

My heart returned to its moorings. We'd soon get them some food, I said. Louisa consulted her wristwatch. 'Ten to twelve,' she observed. 'Just in time for Gingie's minced beef.' It was the next bit that had us licked. 'How clever of you both,' she said, 'to have done all that and Ginger hasn't missed a single meal.'

Ten

We are not the only people odd things happen to, of course, as I was reminded when I was about to start this chapter, by a phone call from a friend.

Sue and her husband Gordon own my favourite dog, an Old English Sheepdog called Pickwick. She also has a Bassenji called Goldie and two cats called Max and Shere Khan. When I answered the phone her voice sounded broken and my heart sank in case it was bad news about my big, mop-headed friend. He has kidney trouble and while the Vet's last report said that Pickwick was currently in better shape than he was and could go on driving them dotty for years, with kidney trouble it is a matter of balance and one can never be sure.

It was all right, Sue assured me hoarsely. It was only that she had flu and had lost her voice. She thought she'd caught it trailing round garages with Gordon, looking for a new car.

'New car?' I said, knowing they'd recently spent a packet on the old one. They'd had to change it, she croaked. The gear-box had now packed in, plus umpteen other things. It just wasn't reliable any more. And their freezer had broken down and the man said it wasn't worth repairing so they'd had to buy a new one. They'd been away when it happened and the contents had all gone soft.

Gosh, I said. How awful. That wasn't the worst of it, she went on. To crown absolutely everything, Goldie had eaten the guinea-pig from next door.

I listened, hardly able to believe my ears. It seemed the little girl next door had wanted to introduce the guinea-pig to Pickwick. Pickwick has that sort of effect. Old ladies dote on him, dour-faced people smile at him – the world is full of Pickwick's friends.

Anyway, apparently the little girl said 'This is Basil, Pickwick,' and held Basil up to the fence and while Pickwick was peering politely through his fringe at him Basil wriggled from her grasp, fell into the garden, and Goldie, the Bassenji hunter, promptly broke Basil's neck. It was a horrifying story, its drama heightened by the fact that Sue was out when it happened. The dogs were in the garden alone, on the other side of the high fence and Goldie, having killed poor Basil, didn't eat him all at once.

There followed a sequence of the utmost high-mindedness – when Sue's next-door neighbour, in spite of what had happened, leaned over the fence flapping frantically with a tea-towel so that Pickwick shouldn't get at the corpse. The fence was too high for her to climb over, she told Sue later, and anyway she was afraid that Goldie might bite – but she knew Pickwick wasn't allowed

meat on account of his kidneys and there was no point in making matters worse.

That was pretty good of her, I said. Sue said it certainly was. They'd replaced the guinea-pig, of course. The very next day, though, Goldie had stolen a joint of pork – the guinea-pig incident having obviously gone to her head – and while Sue, with Pickwick shut indoors for his kidneys' sake, was lecturing her about coming to a bad end, Max had come along, taken the rest of the pork up a tree, Shere Khan had joined him and they'd eaten it.

The sequence of incidents I was about to relate pales in comparison with that. It did all happen the same morning, however, which adds a certain drama to the occasion. It was a morning, shortly after Louisa's return from Canada, when I planned to catch up on a few chores. Clean the upstairs windows; machine the seams on a skirt I was making; and if there was any time left after that, start on mowing the lawn.

I knew it was going to be one of those days when, as I put my arm through the side of the open casement to clean the outside panes, I touched the adjoining shutter and it leaned out from the wall. I grabbed it and shouted for Charles. I hadn't, as he seemed to think when he arrived, been swinging on it. Our shutters don't close. They are purely decorative, each held to the wall by two bolts, and the top bolt had simply come adrift.

Charles examined it. Fortunately there was no need to take the shutter off, he said, but he did wish I'd be more *careful*. He fetched a ladder, mixed some cement, put it in the hole round the bolt. While it set, we supported the shutter with a rope that went from the bed-leg, out through the

window and round to a drain-pipe. It was a good thing I *had* discovered it was loose, I commented. Supposing it had hit somebody on the head? Charles, obviously still convinced I'd been swinging on it, repeated that he hoped I'd be careful from now on. He hadn't time to be always mending things. He wanted to get on with the conservatory.

He didn't get very far with it that morning. I finished the upstairs windows. No more shutters came off. Relieved, I got out the sewing machine and put the seam of my skirt under the foot. I did two measly inches and the whole thing jammed solid, my skirt clamped in immovable teeth.

I do very little sewing and still use Charles's mother's hand machine, which he was able to take apart. He had to, to get my skirt out, though he wasn't very pleased about it. 'How long since you oiled it?' he asked. 'Don't women *ever* read directions? You should oil it every two or three times you use it, not once in twenty years.'

My grandmother used to do that, I said, and got everything she made covered in oil. 'Women and machinery!' said Charles resignedly. '*Now* can I get on with the conservatory?'

Standing on the ladder being tough on his feet, Charles took time off at intervals to rest them. He was, therefore, fortunately indoors with a book when a stone jammed in the lawn-mower a short while later. It wasn't my fault. He will put Annabel on the lawn, saying she likes the grass. She also likes digging holes in it and rolling in them, the lawn being nicely flat. This throws up small stones which are later picked up by the lawnmower, and, being electric, it jams. Usually I can unjam it before Charles heaves into view wearing his Women and Machinery expression, but

this time I'd let the motor run a fraction too long and the stone was wedged as if it had been welded to the machine.

I gave the blades a couple of what I hoped would be quiet taps with a flat stone from the rockery. It sounded as if I was hitting an anvil. Hoping Charles hadn't heard it, I removed the mower to the privacy of the garage and strolled, humming, down past the window to the coal-house. Equally nonchalantly I meandered back a moment later carrying the garden fork as a decoy. Nobody indoors, glancing up from a book, could have seen the coal-hammer I had concealed against my off-side trouser seam. At least, I hoped nobody could.

Up in the garage I hit the mower blade with the coal-hammer and it unjammed at the second attempt. Nonchalantly I strolled back down to the coal-house again – it wouldn't do to leave the evidence around. Charles always gets suspicious when he sees the coal-hammer, it being my usual recourse in an emergency.

I was back on the lawn, the mower going great guns, when Charles came out, his feet refreshed. 'Everything all right?' he enquired, as keeper of the cottage machinery. 'Absolutely fine,' I assured him. 'Good,' beamed Charles benevolently, passing on to the conservatory.

I had spoken too soon. I was cutting the second lawn that afternoon when the flower-arrangement woman turned up. I hadn't seen her since our original encounter but she had said she'd be coming again. I'd learned in the interim that her name was Tomsett and that her husband travelled in ball-bearings. I'd jovially remarked to the Rector's wife, who'd told me, that that must be rather uncomfortable. Alas, it fell on stony ground. 'What must, dear?' she enquired.

Anyway, there was Mrs Tomsett in her feathered hat saying she'd like to speak to me – which meant, since she was speaking to me already, that she expected to be invited indoors: something which, in Siamese households, is not always very convenient.

There can be few Siamese owners who, if they are honest, can say they never have to jump to it when the doorbell rings. To hide, for instance, the favourite possession which somebody insists on keeping on the hearthrug. (When Shebalu was young it was the pot-scourer. Another cat I knew was forever bringing down the bath-sponge.) To whip off the covering bits kept over chair-arms in a desperate attempt to preserve them. In the case of two friends of ours, Dora and Nita, whose home is immaculate, to unpin cellophane protectors from the bottom of their velvet hall curtains.

They have two slant-eyed tyrants, Sugar and Spice, who spray as a means of intimidation. Won't let them out? Right, say the cats, taking up positions against the curtains. As Dora points out, they *have* improved. They used to spray the wall behind the sideboard. They also once sprayed into the control panel on the electric cooker and sabotaged the Sunday lunch. Lately the novelty seems to have worn off a bit. They confine themselves to the curtains. Even so Dora and Nita nearly go mad, pinning on deep cellophane hems when visitors leave, whipping them off when anybody comes, watched by two inscrutable Machiavellis who are likely to spray just for the hell of it the moment the visitors have gone into the sitting-room.

In our case – to revert to Mrs Tomsett – had I known she was coming there were several things I would have done.

Moved the earthbox we kept behind the armchair in the hope of one day persuading Sass to use it, for instance. Whipped up the old rug we kept under the earthbox because, so far, we hadn't. Nipped the vinyl corner-pieces off the carpet in the hall which now looked scruffy as well as peculiar. Shebalu had lately taken to raking at them, when she was shut out, as her own method of trying to get in.

Oh well. It obviously wasn't my day. I ushered Mrs Tomsett in. Actually she overlooked the corner-pieces, her eye caught by the flower arrangement on the carved oak chest. It was a big old tureen filled with lilac and yellow tulips. 'Did you do that?' she asked. I nodded modestly. 'Very *good*,' she said. 'I'm glad my words had some effect.'

As a matter of fact they hadn't. I did that arrangement every spring. In a tureen, because the cats couldn't knock it over. Lilac, because we have loads. The perennial tulips certainly *were* perennial – they were plastic. Some of the best imitations I've seen. Shebalu pulls the petals off real ones and I hate seeing flowers destroyed.

I ushered her into the sitting-room. She heard I wrote, she said as she sat down. She wrote too. Poetry. She must show me some of her work. What she'd really called for, though, was that she'd heard I was opening a boarding cattery. She'd like to help me by leaving Mauritius with me while she and her husband were in Spain. 'I'll give you full instructions about looking after him, of course,' she said, 'seeing that you've had no experience and Mauritius is rather fussy.'

I swallowed, while twenty years of keeping Siamese passed before my eyes. I never did learn why her cat was called Mauritius. I told her we weren't in the boarding business – the house and run were for our own Siamese.

'As for experience,' I said (I knew my voice was rising)...
'when anyone has kept cats as long as we have...'

From experience I should have expected it. At that very
moment Shebalu appeared and got into the earthbox behind
the chair, which undoubtedly Mrs Tomsett wouldn't have
noticed otherwise. She squatted, then began to rise. I knew
what was coming. I leapt forward and held her down.

Mrs Tomsett regarded the pair of us incredulously. Having
finished, Shebalu celebrated by galloping merrily round the
room and Sass appeared from nowhere and joined in. Going
like the clappers, they hurdled Mrs Tomsett's outstretched
legs, leaving her nylons neatly laddered as they passed.

Actually it was fitting retribution, better than any reply
I could have made, but as Mrs Tomsett got up and made
her exit, saying that quite obviously she'd made a mistake,
I did wish that just sometimes the cats didn't let us down,
particularly when it came to sitting in earthboxes.

We hadn't finished yet, however. Going through the hall,
Mrs Tomsett glanced again at my flower arrangement.
Stopped. Went over to touch one of the tulips. 'Plastic!' she
said. 'Plastic *tulips*! I might have known it!' With which she
departed through the door.

When I told Charles about it, he said 'A Day In The Life
Of A Racing Pigeon.' It is one of his favourite comments.
Goodness knows what it means. Charles's sayings are apt
to be somewhat abstract, like 'Needs must when the Devil
drives the barrel-organ.' But this time it sounded most apt.

Eleven

Fortunately things settled down quite quietly for a while after that. Shebalu didn't, as I was afraid she might, start spraying in earnest again. Charles said she'd obviously recognised Mrs Tomsett as a cat and she'd just been warning her off – subtle when you analyse it, if not very complimentary to cats. Charles himself, between brilliant remarks, continued repairing the conservatory, pointing out when I asked about the dresser that it was time now for outdoor work. I wouldn't need the dresser during the summer, he said. We'd be off most of the time in the caravan.

The caravan. How I'd looked forward to it on those winter nights when, seated by a blazing log fire, I'd gone through the caravan magazines a friend had lent us, read useful hints out to Charles and imagined us, foot-loose and self-contained, bowling gaily along the road. There is

something of the nomad in most people, and in Charles and me more than most. One of the most marvellous trips we had ever done had been six weeks in Canada with a camper, when we cooked meals in the open, spent our nights by lonely mountain lakes, and lay awake in the moonlight listening for the rustling that meant bears were about. Now we had a caravan in England. We could go off whenever we liked. 'All of us,' I'd say, putting my arms round the cats curled comfortably on my lap. 'Isn't it going to be fun?' Which was not quite how it struck me now that spring was approaching and I got down to considering it in earnest.

Where would they sleep? With me in my sleeping bag, I could bet on it. Any time they came to bed with us in the cottage it was my shoulder they always made for. Sass insisted on First Place, which was under my chin, and would tread heavily over Shebalu to get it. Shebalu would take umbrage and leave the bed, only to return and poke me in the face a few minutes later. I'd lift up the bedclothes and let her in and the circuit would start all over again, Charles meanwhile snoring soundly away at my side which was why they wouldn't sleep on him... One way and another I didn't get much rest, and that was why we usually shut them downstairs. There was nowhere to shut them in a caravan. I wouldn't get any sleep at all...

I imagined them prowling round the caravan looking up at the rooflight. We must remember to keep that closed. I visualised Sass at work on the store cupboard when we were out. Sass has paws like jemmies. Any door that has a push-catch he can open within minutes. Leaving him for hours with a food cupboard didn't bear thinking about. Neither did the problem of his earthbox. Where were we

going to keep it? There was a lavatory compartment in the caravan but I couldn't see him using it in there. His oracle would probably decide it had to be on Charles's bed and we'd have another clash of temperaments.

We hauled the caravan out of its shed into Annabel's new field so that we could get it ready for the road. We quite often put Annabel in there to graze as well, on a tether as we hadn't yet done the fencing. Inevitably the rumour went round the village that we were going to use Annabel to pull it. Equally inevitably we had to reassure Miss Wellington that nothing was further from our thoughts and in any case it had to be towed by a *car*. Sometimes, said Charles... just sometimes... it would be nice if people got things straight. Meanwhile we were gathering information about other people holidaying with cats.

There was the man, for instance, who came past one afternoon while I was cleaning the caravan windows. (Charles had replaced the broken one and made a perfect job of it.) Was I the one who kept the Siamese? he asked. I said with feeling that I was. Did I take them with us in the caravan? He imagined that it was ours... We'd bought it to take them with us, I said, but I was just realising the snags. Snags? he said. There weren't any. They always took their Siamese with them.

All I can say is, there are cats and cats and anyway he had only one. I listened fascinated while he told the tale of how a balanced Siamese behaves. Ching, he said, was used to a collar and lead. (So were ours, I nodded.) For his sake they didn't tour around with the van – they took it somewhere and left it in one place. For a couple of days they exercised him around the caravan field on his lead, releasing him to

run ahead of them as they neared the van. When he knew exactly where it was and raced to sit outside the door, they could then let him out for exercise on his own, knowing that he'd always come back.

They'd never had to look for him? I asked. He said Ching was too fond of his food. (So were our two. So Seeley had been. But I'd never trust to that again.) What about when they went out? I enquired. Oh, Ching stayed in the caravan and slept. They left the windows slightly open, of course, in case it should get too hot... (I thought of Sass and his jemmy paws and likewise wrote off that one.)

Earthbox? Outside under the caravan. Ching was accustomed to using the garden. At night they put a box in the lavatory compartment but he never got up to use it. Where did he sleep? In the wardrobe. He liked to lie on in the morning and that way they didn't disturb him when they got up and dismantled the bed. He was sure, said the man, that we'd find it easy to cope and that the cats would enjoy coming with us. I bet they would. Whether we could cope was a different matter. My doubts loomed larger and larger...

We had two other testimonials in favour of taking them. One was from a schoolteacher who wrote saying that for years she'd taken her Siamese to Scotland in a motor caravan. The cat got really excited when the van was being packed and tore up and down the stairs. She used to take her climbing in a rucksack until Jan (the cat) became too heavy. She'd now retired and was about to move to Scotland – presumably because Jan enjoyed it.

The other testimonial we were given first-hand when a motor caravan parked outside the cottage one Saturday

afternoon. A girl got out and went round the back – to get her walking boots, I presumed. I was cutting the grass (the mower, touch wood, was going well) and prepared to ask my usual question. Was she likely to be long? If so, would she like to park behind our coal-house because where she was, nobody else could get by. Undoubtedly we live in what looks like an outpost of civilisation but we do have neighbours along a couple of tracks. One of them, a fiery Scot, was in the habit of letting the air out of the obstructer's tyres and then going home leaving his own car behind the first one. The times we'd soothed people, helped them blow up their tyres and rung Angus to come and let them out – his car now blocked theirs, which proved *we* hadn't done it, but it hardly made for a peaceful life.

'Are you...?' I began to say to the girl, then stood there open-mouthed. Many people who have read about the cats and Annabel come to see us, but it was the first time one had brought her Siamese!

We couldn't invite her to bring him in. Our two were already looking at him out of the window. Sass with interest, Shebalu with her ears flattened and her tail up. Her tail up... Oh crumbs, no! I thought in despair. I visualised her marching over to the earthbox, standing up when she thought of the Cheek of It, my not being there to sit her down... Oh well, I thought, smiling brightly, preparing to greet my visitor as a grateful author should.

After we'd chatted for a while and she'd seen our two through the window she asked if she could exercise Simba up on the hill. Of course, I said, but if she'd excuse me I'd better go in. Our two would be getting awfully jealous.

They already were. Shebalu was on the piano, swearing horribly with her eyes crossed. Sass had his tail bushed. It only bushes above the bent bit and looks all the more fearsome for that. I was still soothing them down when the girl returned, put Simba in the van and drove off. We'd already said goodbye so there was no need for me to go out. Which was why, seeing a stranger putting a Blue Point Siamese into a van right outside our cottage with neither Charles nor I in sight, Tim Bannett thought it was somebody kidnapping Shebalu and was hammering on our door within seconds.

He'd spotted the incident as he was coming down from his field and had scratched the number of the van in the dust. Pretty smart thinking. Had it really been Shebalu we'd have got her before she left the county. If only Tim had been around the morning that Seeley went out... As it was, Charles came up with a new hazard. Supposing somebody fancied them if we left them in the caravan in a camping field and forced the door and carried them off?

You'd think, from the complexities we thought up, that they were a pair of priceless diamonds. To us, of course, they were, added to which there was always the thought of Seeley, which made us so much more wary than most. I remembered a story Pauline Furber told me when I'd rung her to ask about having a kitten. She'd quoted it to reassure me that lost cats often do get found – that while she thought Sass was made to measure for us, Seeley might still come back.

It seemed that some people from Manchester took their Siamese queen to a caravan site near Weymouth and halfway through the fortnight she disappeared. They searched

for her, put up notices in the local shops, extended their holiday – but in the end they'd had to go home, asking the site-owner to contact them if there was any news, though by then they had little hope. The season ended, the winter passed – it was the bad winter of 1967. Even in Dorset the conditions were arctic. There was no hope at all now, thought her owners.

It was nearly a year later that Pauline's mother-in-law, who lived near the site, saw a slender tail and black-stockinged legs going past her sitting-room door. Food had been vanishing from her kitchen for some time, though she had never previously managed to spot the culprit. She called her son. They went to the door and peered round the corner. It was a Siamese all right. Thin but fit-looking, with a coat that had thickened like a bear's – proof that it had lived out all the winter. It was carrying a fillet of haddock in its mouth. The son followed it across several fields. There, watching a family of kittens devour the fish, under a tree-root in a hedge, was undoubtedly the missing Siamese.

He crept quietly away and told the owner of the caravan site, who phoned the people in Manchester at once. They drove down the same day. It was their cat, all right. She came when they called as though she hadn't been away for more than five minutes, bellowing a greeting, making a fuss of them, inviting them to Come and see what She'd Got. They took her back to Manchester, black and white kittens and all, saying they intended to keep the lot of them. Whether that had been the reason she'd wandered off – that she was in season and looking for a mate (though this wouldn't have been the original litter, there must have been a lot of half-Siamese around). Whether she'd simply felt the

call of the wild as some Siamese seem to – we'd heard of so many who'd vanished from their homes and been found safe and well months later, having walked in on some other family with an air of condescension and just taken over the place... her owners were lucky; they'd got her back, thanks to a glimpse of a tail going past a doorway.

Pauline had told us this story when we first met her, before we'd ever thought of having a caravan. I'd forgotten it in the interim but now it came back with a bang. Supposing our two managed to get out of the caravan despite our taking all precautions? Enlarged the hole round the sink-pipe, for instance, or managed to prise open one of the windows? The window over the cooker wasn't a very tight fit. I could just see Sass sitting there winkling it open. I visualised the pair of them disappearing across a field themselves, one long bent black tail accompanied by a small but valiant blue one. Our coming back to find them gone. The frantic search. The months of wondering. Two little cats living wild in a wood. Winter coming on. The pair of them cold and hungry... My imagination was building it up into an *Orphans of the Storm* scenario when Sass singed his feet on the cooker and my mind was definitely made up.

He was mooching round the kitchen one morning when I took a pot off the stove. Normally he isn't allowed in the kitchen while I'm cooking, but somehow I'd overlooked him. Realising, presumably by ESP since he couldn't see it, that there was now a vacant space on the stove-top where it might be advantageous to stand, he took off from the floor in one of his leaps, straight for the red-hot ring. Fortunately I saw him coming and have learned to be fast-moving from long experience. As I raised the saucepan and his head appeared

underneath, much as I hated doing it I knocked him flying with the other. He vanished under the table wailing that I'd Hit Him, in a strong aroma of singed Sass. He was quite all right, though. His pads weren't even blistered. Only the hair around them was scorched. But if he could do that in the kitchen, what could happen in the caravan, with gas rings, not much room and two of them about the place? It was no good, I said. My nerves wouldn't stand it. For our first trip, at any rate, we'd *have* to board the cats.

How lucky we were. When I rang Pauline Furber to ask if she knew of anyone she could recommend she said she could take them herself if we liked. People had asked her so often that she'd just put up three houses and runs especially to take her own ex-kittens when their owners went on holiday.

I could hardly believe it. She understood Siamese as thoroughly as the Francises did and loved the kittens she bred so much that, when we bought Sass from her she'd said that if Seeley did come back and we didn't want Sass any more, would we let her have him back, not pass him on to anyone else. I had assured her that Sass was ours for good, whether Seeley came back or not. Not for nothing had he wrapped that small bent tail around my heart as soon as I saw him. Not for nothing had he fixed me with his strange, hypnotic stare. The stare he still, as a grown cat, uses on occasion when he wants to bend me to his will, such as when sitting between me and the television he decides it is his bedtime and tries by telepathy to make me get His Milk, and hurry up and hand over His Chair...

Yes, the houses were separate, Pauline assured me. And they did have locks on the doors. And the runs *were* paved

so they couldn't tunnel under... Had I forgotten she had Sass's father, and that several of the kittens she boarded were his? Built like Alcatraz was her motto, and it would be nice for Sass to see his Dad.

When we aimed the caravan up the hill a few weeks later watched by a group of interested neighbours – most of them were at the bottom, ready to push, but Miss Wellington appeared to be praying at the top – at least we didn't have to worry about the cats. They were safe with Pauline at Burrowbridge.

Twelve

We made it. Eyes closed, gripping the edge of my seat, I just about willed that caravan up. There was a tense moment halfway up the hill when Charles stopped to check that he could take off again. He did it at the behest of one of our friends, who said if we could take off from standstill there we could take off on anything. He'd eat his lunch with a much better conscience, he said, if he didn't have a vision of us somewhere on a hill going backwards.

It was a wonder his vision wasn't realised there and then. It felt as if we were being held by a heavy anchor. I was wondering at which point we ought to jump – then once more we were moving upwards. Past Miss Wellington – hands clasped, eyes closed. Round the corner by the Rose and Crown. The landlord came out to wish us *Bon Voyage* and see that we didn't hit his wall.

On round the bend, in more ways than one. Through the main part of the village. It was a Saturday morning and there were quite a few people about, glancing at the car and recognising us. Charles said did I *have* to look as if I was airborne at thirty thousand feet? I attempted to relax... to smile graciously at them, like the Queen. It wasn't an easy task. I don't suppose she'd feel much like smiling, either, towing a caravan for the first time behind her coach.

The friend who'd lent us the magazines was right, though – after half an hour we hardly realised it was there. Our confidence grew with every minute of the journey down to Dorset and we drove into the camping field with aplomb. It was a Caravan Club Certified Location site – one of their small, five-caravan-only ones, which we had looked at some weeks before. It had seemed ideal for our initial try out, with its left-hand turn-in that led through an ample gateway and along a wide, well-gravelled track. There was plenty of room on the flat, grassy site, too. It would be the easiest thing in the world to park.

Overcome by the success of our journey, Charles announced that he would now back into place. He hadn't backed a caravan before. Equally overcome I got out to direct him, trying to look as though we'd been doing it for years. I was so impressed with the skill with which he was managing it – it is quite a difficult business, one has to turn the steering wheel in what would normally be the wrong direction to start with and it's easy to jack-knife the whole thing, but there was the caravan, as if by magic, gliding expertly into line – that I failed to notice the black smoke pouring from under the car until one of the other caravanners came running up.

'You've got the caravan brake on,' he shouted. 'This your first time out? We all do that at the start.'

I should have remembered that the caravan brake goes on automatically when the car is in reverse. It is a safety measure, to hold the caravan if anything goes wrong on a hill. If you want to back the caravan the brake lever has to be held up by an assistant, or fixed with an elastic band. It was my job, I'd forgotten it in the excitement of the moment, and Charles had been reversing nearly a ton of caravan against the force of its very efficient brakes.

When I asked if it mattered, Charles said not so you'd really notice it. We'd probably ruined the clutch. No doubt burnt out the brake linings, too, but what was a little thing like that? He gave a hollow laugh and kicked the caravan wheels. At least they didn't fall off.

Actually our car is pretty tough and it didn't appear to have done it any harm. When I rang Pauline she said the cats were alright too, and eating like little pigs. Yes, she was feeding Sass separately. She saw what I meant about his being a gannet. (Sass not only ate twice as fast as Shebalu, he'd also perfected a system of bolting the first part of his own meal, looking across at Shebalu's dish and deciding that she had More, nipping over and grabbing half of it in one mighty Sass-sized mouthful, then scooting like lightning back to his.)

No, she said, he hadn't blotted his copybook. (I'd warned her about his obsession with wool. He hadn't wet his blanket for a good while now but there was no knowing when he might start. Away from home, where he could let us down thoroughly, would be an obvious incentive to him, particularly if he decided that *not* doing it was

the reason he was there.) He was using his box as good as gold, said Pauline. Butter wouldn't melt in his mouth. As for Shebalu, she was a poppet – exactly like her Dad. (Valentine, Shebalu's Champion of Champions father, had also been one of Pauline's cats.)

So, content that they were in good hands and that hopefully the clutch and brake linings had survived, we spent our experimental week in Dorset. Charles liked caravanning so much he got carried away and bought a recorder to play in the evenings. This was the life, he said, pausing between piercing blasts while a cow answered him from over the hedge. The gipsy spirit. The feeling of freedom. Why hadn't we done this before? He reckoned he could compose on this recorder. He hadn't felt so inspired for years.

That wasn't what he said at the end of the week when, on our way back to the cottage, we found ourselves going the wrong way through Langport. I was navigating and had missed the turning. I realised as soon as we'd passed it. But you can't pull a caravan outfit into the side of the road and reverse it as you would a car. We had to go on, down the steep winding hill into the main street, which in Langport is very narrow. There was traffic building up behind us, traffic coming towards us... What the hell, demanded Charles, did we do *now*?

'Take the next turning left,' I said. Charles frantically swung the wheel. We found ourselves in a cul-de-sac in front of some garages. Charles said he couldn't reverse the caravan there, either, unless I fancied one that looked like a concertina.

There was only one thing for it – to unhitch the caravan and turn it round by hand. We could just reverse the car on

its own. And while we were heaving at the coupling and covering ourselves with grease (the book said to lubricate the tow-hitch liberally and Charles always takes instructions at their word) a gang of small children materialised from nowhere and squatted down to watch us with interest.

'That your caravan?' one enquired.

'Yes, it is,' I said.

'Why did you bring it up this lane?'

'To turn it round,' I told him.

'What do you want to turn it round for?'

'So we can go the other way.'

'Why do you want to go the other way?'

'WHY DO YOU THINK!' I said. Which was why, as a lesson to me to be patient in future with innocent, enquiring youth – as I bent with Charles over the two-bar, struggling to heave the hitch into position, several handfuls of gravel hit me on the seat of my slacks and a chorus of little voices said 'Yah!'

All it needed after that was for us to go on to Burrowbridge, having arranged to collect the cats on the way, to learn that halfway through the week Sass had gone on strike against his box and had been using a hole in the paving of his run instead. It was hardly more than a crack, where a small stone had come out. Pauline said the accuracy of his aim was quite amazing. He sat on it looking so earnest, too, as though he was performing some sort of rite. He was, I said, though goodness knew what it was. All we could do was be thankful that he hadn't performed it on his blanket.

Things didn't change much, did they? said Charles as we drove home across the moors. Siamese just existed to let one down. They thought up things one couldn't possibly

imagine. Who would have expected that addle-pated cat to use a crack in the paving as a lavatory?

Who, either, could have envisaged the trouble we were to have at the cottage when he evolved an even better system of opening doors – to the extent that we had to keep the back one locked because we kept finding him swinging from the handle, with Shebalu sitting beside him with her paws folded waiting for Genius to let them out?

That one was easily taken care of by our locking the door, of course. It was the doors we couldn't lock that were the trouble. The pull-down flap in front of the cooker grill, for instance, which had foxed our other cats for years. I used to put things in there from the freezer when I wanted to thaw them out. The first time I found the conspirators in the kitchen gnawing a half-thawed chop between them, I thought I must have forgotten to close it. I removed the cats, got out another chop, grilled the chewed one for them for their own lunch... *separately*, on a piece of *foil*, I assured Charles, who is particular about germs...

The next day I found them chewing at a string of sausages and this time I *knew* I hadn't left the grill door open. I decided to keep watch. I replaced the sausages, closed the flap and took the cats with me into the sitting-room. After a moment or two Sass departed nonchalantly in the direction of the kitchen. Equally nonchalantly Shebalu followed him. Creeping across to peer through the door-crack, I saw the ultimate in cat co-operation.

Reaching up on his spindly back legs, Sass hooked the grill flap down with one pull. He did it as one who had practised it, putting his paw in at one side, no amateurish fumbling about with the handle. Shebalu, who'd been watching him

from the top of the cooker, now got down on the flap and crawled inside on her stomach. She is smaller than Sass and the pair of them had obviously worked out that this was her part of the job. She backed out carrying the sausages, which she dropped to the floor with a frozen thud. Sass moved in to tackle them, she jumped down to join him... till then they'd worked like a couple of commandos, but at that point natural instinct took over. He growled at her and said the sausages were His and she hit him on the nose.

They carried out this joint technique at every opportunity after that and I had to give up thawing meat in the grill compartment. For a while I used the oven instead, but it so happens that I make my own bread and I kept putting in liver, for instance, forgetting it was there, and then later I'd turn on the oven, ready to bake the bread... I fused so many helpings of liver to their polystyrene trays I could almost have started a glue factory.

I next switched to thawing things in one of the wall cupboards but still Sass the Sleuth was on the trail. I'd find him reared up like a Lippizaner, his front legs poised in mid-air, sniffing at the door of whichever cupboard I'd chosen while his Blue Point accomplice looked on. Take those two in a caravan with us? We'd be asking for everything we got!

Sass illustrated that, when I took them into the caravan parked in Annabel's field one day, by immediately hooking open all the cupboards one after another. Kid's Stuff, he informed me complacently, going off to sit in the doorway and impress passers-by with the fact that the van was All His. Shebalu was meanwhile busy trying to lift one of the mattresses, so she could get into the space underneath.

How she knew there was a space there was beyond me, but to save the mattress from demolition I held it up.

She got in. From there she couldn't see Sass, who was hidden from her view by the corner of the wardrobe, but immediately behind him, on the floor where she could see it, was the handle used to wind down the caravan supports. I'd put it there to remind me that we had to wind them up again before we did any towing. Dire things could happen if we didn't. It was made of half-inch-thick black iron and it was right-angled. It hadn't interested Sass in the least. But Shebalu was staring at it as if she was mesmerised. What did she think it was, I wondered. A snake?

Sass reappeared, having tired of sitting in the doorway. She eyed him intently as he passed. She stared at his rear... back at the handle... and I suddenly realised what it was. She'd thought it was his tail. That, too, is black and right-angled. She'd been wondering what it was doing there all by itself.

Shebalu is super-observant. It was she who, when I was with them on the lawn one evening, spotted movement in a patch of moss under the lilac tree and promptly sat down to watch. Probably a field-mouse, I thought, getting ready to grab her if she jumped. We don't let the cats kill things if we can help it and we were particularly vigilant that summer because Lancelot was presumably somewhere around. He'd left his quarters in the kitchen in the spring, it was odds on he was still in the garden, and Charles said he had a lot of nuts invested in Lancelot and we didn't want him being eaten.

When the moss and bits of twig finished their slow-motion heaving, however, it wasn't Lancelot who emerged.

I watched, my eyes as round as Shebalu's, as what looked like a snout came out. Grey, wrinkled... like a miniature elephant's trunk. The similarity struck me immediately. I held Shebalu by the collar – whatever it was might be dangerous. Sass was with us now, peering over Shebalu's back. Even as we watched, what looked like two African elephant's ears appeared – grey, wide at the top, with a striking flaming-pink lining. I guessed then what it was, though I'd never seen one before. Obviously an elephant hawk moth, emerging from its chrysalis in our lawn.

I called Charles and we transferred it for safety to the flower border, putting it gently on a delphinium leaf. Shebalu, having watched its emergence, took no further interest in it, but Sass kept prowling around, testing the air with the exaggeratedly questing sniffs that are another of his attributes. Sass has the strongest sense of smell I have ever known.

We kept an eye on the moth. Its wings unfolded within the hour. They were camouflage grey on top but I bent to look underneath and there the back ones still had their pink colour. The pink was becoming fainter now, as it dried out having served its purpose of emphasising the 'ears' of the moth as it emerged, still weak, from its chrysalis and persuading any potential enemy that it was an elephant.

It had gone next day. But for Shebalu we would never have seen it. There probably aren't many people who've watched an elephant hawk moth hatch out. The cats certainly did help bring nature home to us. But... take them with us in the caravan?

Sass settled that question with his own item of nature study. Again I was with them on the lawn. It was evening

and Sass, his big ears stuck up like barge sails on the Norfolk Broads, was watching a patch of grass against the wall.

By midsummer our lawn is always surrounded with what looks like the African bush where I can't get the mower close up to the wall. We always mean to cut the edge with the shears, but we never do. Neither of us can ever find the time. Eventually it reaches the stage where we say it would be a pity to cut it, the cats like hunting in it so much. Then, of course, we have to watch them more closely than ever, to make sure that what they do catch they don't kill...

Both cats had their long nylon leads on. It was almost dusk and I wasn't risking their getting away. So, when Sass pounced and came out carrying the smallest of shrews, I relieved him of it in a second. With Sass it is just a matter of picking him up and he drops whatever he has at once. He holds it very lightly – he has a mouth like a retriever – it only has to wriggle and it has escaped. This one fell on the close-cut grass in the middle of the lawn, scuttled wildly around for a moment looking for cover and, failing to find any, went to earth under the instep of one of my rubber clogs. I put them on when I take the cats out after it has been raining, for I never know when I'm going to be led through mud and they are easy to slip on and off.

I knelt down, my main thought being to give more cover to the shrew. Not only was Sass busy looking for it, but Shebalu was also casting around. She is like lightning, that one. She'd get the shrew if he didn't, once it came out.

I shouted for Charles. 'Sass has caught a shrew!' I yelled. 'I've got it under my clog.'

'Under where?' asked Charles, coming at the double. 'What's he been up to now?'

It was at that moment that an awful thought struck me. I was kneeling down. If the shrew came out from under my instep, it could go straight up the leg of my slacks! I leapt up hurriedly, flattening my right foot which, while I was kneeling, I'd half bent out of my clog. I let out a scream.

'What's the matter?' asked Charles.

'It's in my clog!' I yelled.

It was too. The cats watched round-eyed as, with Charles holding them back, I hopped across the lawn, tipped my clog over the long grass and an extremely angry shrew fell out.

That shrew was pretty quick-thinking, said Charles. It certainly was, I said. I'd been doing a bit of thinking too, and I'd come to a definite conclusion. What with Shebalu and her nature studies and Sass's shrews getting in my clogs and his genius for opening cupboards... In due course we'd take them caravanning. There was nothing I'd like better. But until we got them trained to behave like normal cats, they were going under lock and key at Burrowbridge with Pauline.

Thirteen

We took the caravan away three times that summer, enjoying it more and more each time we went. 'We *must* start bringing the cats with us,' I kept saying as we relaxed in comfort in it at night. I imagined Shebalu curled on the bunk beside me; Sass gazing wonderingly out at the sea; the pair of them chasing, tails raised, along the seashore if we could find a beach without dogs.

'No reason why we shouldn't,' Charles would reply between blissful blasts on his recorder. 'Provided we take all precautions.' At which another panorama would cross my mind. Windows screwed down permanently. Bars across the rooflight. There'd have to be an escape hatch over the door. Even then I could see us coming back one evening to find they'd discovered a way out through the floor. Perhaps we shouldn't be too precipitate after all, I'd say. They were perfectly happy with Pauline. One day, though, when we

could really be sure they were safe, we really *would* bring them along.

We went to Devon for our second trip. It passed off without a hitch. There was nothing to caravanning when you were used to it, we said. We almost *could* have brought the cats. It was out of the question, though, on our third trip, when we took the caravan to Cornwall for three weeks and were joined for part of the time by Louisa and my cousin Dee, who rented a residential caravan a short way from where we had our touring one. Dee has a dog called Rosie who is Nemesis-on-wheels to cats and Louisa can be guaranteed on any occasion to need enough surveillance for fifty. On this particular holiday Louisa kept falling down.

It wasn't, as she told us when we picked her up, that she was getting old. She isn't anything like old to start with and in any case looks twenty years younger. It was the fault of a pair of trendy shoes she'd bought and absolutely insisted on wearing.

They had walking tops, she said, defensively displaying the Oxford laces when we told her they were lethal. So they might, but they didn't have walking soles. They also had stack heels like woodpiles in a log-yard and she clumped along on them as if she was perched on pattens. We'd complained last year when she wore her boots, she went on. That was true enough. While Charles, Dee and I went round in proper walking boots, Louisa had worn her fleece-lined winter ones. Not only did they look odd on a cliff-path in September, with butterflies still on the ragwort and the Cornish sun blazing down, but she'd stumbled several times over the bulky toes and we automatically

closed round her like fielders in a cricket match when she got near the edge of a cliff.

This year, with her stack heels, it was worse than ever. She fell down even when the ground was flat. Louisa tripping over nothing carrying a bucket of water was practically a daily occurrence at the camp.

It wasn't funny when she fell on the rocks at Kynance, however. Louisa was considerably shaken. Perhaps she *should* get some boots after all, she said. Walking ones like ours. So Dee drove her over to Penzance and what did she have when she returned? A pair of ski boots. She said she'd liked the look of them, and they were waterproof and would be useful in the garden.

How that suited them for cliff walking was clear only to Louisa, but there she was, trudging happily along wearing ski boots in September. They were black, square-toed and had bright yellow piping; people looked with curiosity when they saw them. On warm days, Louisa said they were hot, which wasn't surprising, but at least she didn't fall down in them. She hadn't discarded the stack heels, though. They were still to have their moment.

Charles and I had gone to Cornwall a fortnight ahead of Dee and Louisa and we came back a few days earlier. I asked Louisa if there was anything I could do for her when we got back and she said would I ring her brother. He is a widower, lives alone and thinks the world of Louisa. Like her, he is also somewhat woolly. Told she'd be away for a fortnight, he'd thought she'd said a week and had stocked up her larder for her return. He'd written to tell her so and Louisa had had a fit... he always bought steak for Ginger, she said, and when I said well, if he was as bonkers as that

at least he could put it in her freezer – Oh no, she said. He wouldn't do that. He knew Ginger liked it fresh. He'd probably thrown it out.

Anxious there shouldn't be a repeat and that he should know exactly when she was coming back, she asked me to tell him she'd be home on Monday night and would he please leave the garden door unbolted. After considerable heart-searching she'd been persuaded to leave Ginger at a very good cattery near Bristol, she and Dee were going to collect him on the way, and she wanted to go in through the garden door because it was easier for carrying his basket.

I rang my uncle. He said he was sorry to hear about the back door because it would be dark when she got home. He'd done a few odd jobs for her while she was away, including laying a new garden path. It had taken more cement than he'd calculated, however, and there was still an eight-foot strip unfinished at the end...

'Oh crumbs!' I gasped. 'And she'll come in in the dark and go headlong over the edge!'

Oh no, he said blissfully. She'd be able to *see* it. There was light enough from the street lamp for that. It was just that if she'd come through the front way in daylight she'd have then gone out to look at the garden, and the path would have been a nice surprise for her and she would have seen it from the finished end.

I worried. I worried all the weekend. I wasn't a bit surprised when Louisa rang me on Monday night to announce that she was home, Ginger was fine and she'd just fallen down on the path.

'No dear, not at that end,' she said as I breathed fire and slaughter about my uncle. It seemed she'd come through

the back door, spotted the break in the path as he had forecast, carried Ginger safely indoors... She'd then gone out with a torch to have a better look and had fallen flat over nothing at the top.

That wasn't all. I can't ring Louisa because she refuses to have a phone. She says it would startle her when it rang, Ginger wouldn't like it either, and supposing she got rude calls? She rings me instead, from the callbox in her road, and we are forever having alarms when Louisa can't get her tuppence in and we are cut off in mid-call, or I hear bangs in the background, or people's voices, and I ask what is going on. 'Somebody wants to use it,' she says. 'Well dear, I'd better go.' She then hangs up immediately, leaving me having a fit at my end in case somebody has biffed her on the head.

The night she came home from holiday her call finished abruptly as usual and the next day Charles and I drove into town. I was afraid she might have felt peculiar after her fall and I'd been worrying about her all night. No, she hadn't felt giddy, she said. It was just that there were several other people waiting for the phone. As a matter of fact, though, as she was coming out of the callbox the woman who was next in the queue had pushed in – it hadn't left Louisa much room to manoeuvre and she *had* fallen down again.

'It was the dog,' she said as I clutched my head and told her she must be more careful.

'Which dog?' I enquired. The dog being held by the next person in the phone queue, apparently. Louisa had tripped over his lead. She'd fallen flat on the dog – winding him so he could only squeak, she said, and he'd realised she was cross with him because when she got up, his ears

were down. She'd told his owner he ought to control his damned dog and marched home in high dudgeon. It was dreadful language for Louisa. She must indeed have been feeling shaken.

She'd then lain awake all night, loving animals as she does, worrying whether she'd upset the dog by what she said or hurt him when she landed on him. 'His poor ears were so *down,*' she kept saying. 'I wish I hadn't spoken so crossly.' Some dogs have their ears down naturally, I comforted her. What sort of little dog was he? I'd imagined something pint-sized. Being Louisa I should have known. She was jolly lucky he *had* only squeaked. She'd fallen on a whacking great Alsatian.

She had, we discovered when we questioned her, been wearing those confounded stack heels. She thought they'd be all right for town, she said. Other people wore them. Not people with a centre of gravity like hers, we told her, firmly relieving her of them.

So the caravan was a success, Louisa wasn't getting old and the cats had been fine at Pauline's. They'd spent three holidays at Burrowbridge by this time and were obviously quite at home there. On their second visit, to make them even more so, I'd taken along a large clump of grass in a pot. They were going to be there for a fortnight and while there was grass along the wire of their run – enough, as Pauline said, for normal cats – as I explained, our two eat a great deal of grass and one could hardly describe them as normal.

'How right you are,' she'd said when I rang her from Devon. 'Do you know what that cat has done now?' 'That cat' is always Sass, of course. Shebalu invariably behaves

herself when away from home. Teacher's favourite hoping for merit marks has nothing on our canny blue girl.

At first, it seemed, they had eaten the grass, then Sass had taken to sitting on it. It had turned yellow, he'd then given up the hole in the paving and adopted the grass pot as an earthbox instead. She wouldn't have minded, Pauline said, but he had an outsize box in his house. What on earth made him perch on a flowerpot? Did we think he was right in the head?

She was the one who'd raised him, I told her... Personally I thought it was part of his ritual. He was probably trying to ensure that the weather stayed fine, or that he got rabbit again for his supper. Pauline gave them a lot of fresh rabbit and they once went on strike when she didn't.

He used the grass pot as an earthbox the next time he went there, too. It obviously *had* become part of his ritual. Pauline said she was getting used to him now. He just wasn't like other cats. Even so, why he took a toad into their sleeping accommodation is something we puzzle over still.

It must have been Sass. Shebalu wouldn't have touched it. He is the only one who carries strange things round in his mouth. When I picked up their travelling basket, anyway, there was the toad behind it, goggling at us as large as life. Pauline said it couldn't have gone in on its own because the weather had been chilly and she'd kept the door of their sleeping quarters shut. She'd had the heater on and the cats had gone in and out through the slightly open window which was a good four feet up from the ground. No toad, she said, could have jumped straight up in the air and in through a small gap like that. There was somebody else who could have done it, though, carrying the toad in his

mouth... But why on earth would he want to? I asked. If there was one thing she didn't like it was toads, she said, and whether that little devil knew it... She wouldn't put anything past him.

Oddly enough, the following summer we found a large toad in the run of the cat house at the cottage. It couldn't have got through the small-gauge wire and it certainly hadn't gone in through the door, which we never leave open, even when the cats aren't in the run, for fear of birds getting in. There was the toad, though, trying futilely to climb the wire on the inside while Sass sat interestedly beside it. Charles brought it out and put it on the garden by the garage, leaving it to make its own way. It could have gone anywhere in the Valley – but where did we find it next morning? Or rather, where did Sass find it, with that incredible nose of his? Back by their run, huddled forlornly against the outside of the frame, as if the one thing it wanted was to get in.

We didn't let it. A toad needs a wider range than a cat-run. Besides which Sass was prodding it energetically through the bars, which hardly augured a congenial relationship, though it didn't seem to worry the toad. I covered it with leaves to stop him annoying it, leaving a hole through which it could breathe. It stayed there all day, looking out from its shelter like a contemplative hermit, withdrawing slightly when I bent down to look at it.

Next day it had gone. We never saw it again. We wondered, though – had Sass some affinity with toads? How did two of them come to be with him in places where it was logically impossible for them *to* be – and why did the second one try to get back?

If Sass knew, he wasn't telling. There is much that is mysterious about that cat. In any case, when we'd got back from Cornwall the previous autumn we'd had other things than toads on our minds. We found that the Valley had been invaded by what a friend termed The Pheasants' Revolt.

They came from a nearby estate whose coverts had lain empty for years until, with syndicate shooting becoming popular, the owner had let the rights to a tenant who had started raising pheasants there again. We'd seen them in their runs when we took Annabel out for exercise and had felt sorry when we thought of their fate. True they wouldn't have been bred if it hadn't been for that purpose, but we hated to think of anything being shot.

Apparently so did the pheasants. They'd been released from their runs while we were away on holiday, to get used to flying before the shooting season started, and it looked, when we got back from Cornwall, as if most of them had come to live with us. They sat in their dozens on our wall. They strutted about with Annabel on the hillside. They meandered about picking grit up in the lane. We had to absolutely crawl up the hill when we took the car out because they kept flying out in front of the bonnet.

One theory was that the hillside where they'd been raised was too cold for them now it was autumn, and that when they were freed they had naturally made for the shelter of the Valley. The man who'd raised them still put corn out every night up at the runs but Fred Ferry said pheasants was wily. They seemed to know about guns by instinct and a lot of 'em would make off while the going was good.

Maybe so – but why come to us? I asked. Fred explained that we were right by the stream. "'N thee bist right on

the edge of the wood, and thee hassn't got a dog and 'tis quiet as the grave down here.' ''Cept when thic cat of thine starts up,' he amended, looking across the lawn at Sass who, probably with Fred's sherry in mind, was bawling matily at him from the cat-run.

'Theest know what?' he said, suddenly inspired, 'Theest ought to put down some corn theeself. Then theest could let out thic cat... By gorry, he 'ouldn't 'alf be useful...'

'Oh no he wouldn't,' I said.

Fred muttered to himself all the way up the hill, but we wouldn't have dreamed of doing any such thing. In particular we wouldn't have let Sass chase Phyllis who, within days of our coming home, had adopted us.

She was the smallest, drabbest, scrawniest pheasant hen you could ever expect to see, but she had the assurance of a Salvation Army bandswoman. You could well imagine her banging a tambourine as she approached with her deliberate, slow-stalking tread. She did approach us, too, unlike the showier, posturing cock-pheasants who flapped away, squawking their heads off, the moment we got anywhere near them. I only had to open the door to shake out the tablecloth and Phyllis would stroll quietly, unhurriedly, up.

I could shake the cloth right over her, Phyllis didn't mind; nor was she the least bit concerned about Sass. She must have worked out what his being on a lead meant and when I opened the door to take them out and he shot out like a greyhound from a trap – silently, as was Sass the Mighty Hunter's wont – she knew he couldn't get far. She merely slow-stepped on to the lawn till she was sure we had him under control, then she'd slow-step nonchalantly back –

141

which was heart-warming in that it meant she trusted us but extremely frustrating to Sass, almost nose to beak with a Siamese's idea of heaven and held back by a rotten old collar.

She was hungry, said Charles. Look at her thin little body. Probably the other pheasants wouldn't let her eat with them. She was obviously attracted to the yard by the crumbs we threw out for the birds, and to us because she knew we put them out. If we put crumbs on the far side of the lawn for her, she wouldn't hang around the door and upset Sass. (Who, when he was indoors, now spent most of his time planning her downfall from the window above the freezer.)

This meant two lots of crumbs, since we couldn't neglect our regulars. It also meant two lots of crumbs for Phyllis, who followed me across the lawn, ate the lot I put down over there, then stalked back to the yard and joined the sparrows.

'Corn,' said Charles inspiredly. 'The packet Louisa brought back from Canada for popping – if we gave that to Phyllis she wouldn't bother about the crumbs – that would keep her away from the door.'

Phyllis appreciated the corn. She waited eagerly for it every morning, following me across the lawn when she saw the packet. Unfortunately when she'd finished that she came back and ate the birds' crumbs anyway and all we had to show for that advancement was that now she expected corn from us as well – how could we stop giving it to her, once we had started? – and Sass was more frustrated than ever. Not only was she mooching unconcernedly around the yard whenever he went out, knowing full well he couldn't get at

her, but if he went across the lawn to his favourite hunting corner with me holding on to his lead, he only had to look round and That Pheasant would be following close behind us, thinking that if I was on the lawn it meant corn.

Other people were beginning to notice her, too, following me around like a domestic hen. Fred Ferry, seeing me throw down the popcorn one morning, said he seed we was following his advice. Oh no we weren't, I said. This one was tame. We were feeding her because she was so thin.

'Thin?' said Fred. I followed his eyes. I'd got used to thinking of her as scrawny, but Phyllis, on a diet of popcorn and bird crumbs, was now sleek-feathered, practically as broad as she was long and ripe for anybody's table.

It was November now and shooting had started. I hoped she would stay safe. The other pheasants gradually disappeared – scared off, perhaps, by the guns. Or they might have eaten what wild food there was and moved on to other grounds. Or gone back to the runs for the corn put out by the keeper and, inevitably, been shot.

Whether Phyllis would escape was in the lap of the gods. I would *not*, I said, grow fond of her. But how could I avoid it – going up, for instance, to clear a bramble patch in Annabel's field and looking up to find her standing quietly watching me. Goodness knows where she had come from; we had no idea where she slept... but when I came back, she followed me down the lane to the cottage, walking like a devoted dog at my heels. Only because she was hoping for corn when we got back, I knew, but how could I *not* get fond of her?

Charles did too. He didn't think she'd go back to the runs, he said. She was too content in the Valley. Certainly

we weren't responsible for her being down here, either – it wasn't our fault she liked the bird crumbs. What he was afraid of was her strolling about in the lane the way she did and somebody coming past and knocking her on the head. He never had liked Fred Ferry's knapsack... Secretly I'd been thinking the same.

We watched over her through November and on into December, nipping out when Fred Ferry appeared. He seemed to be going past more than ever. Even Father Adams noticed it. One of these days that old Fred'd meet hisself coming back, he observed.

After the end of December Phyllis would be safe – from guns, at any rate, since the shooting of hen-pheasants ceases then. As for Fred – he wouldn't dare, I said. He knew I had my eye on him. So Phyllis continued, placidly content. She'd eaten her way through the popcorn. 'Better buy her some more,' said Charles. 'Not to get fond of her, mind, but she seems to have taken us on and we can hardly stop feeding her now.'

Six days before Christmas I bought her a seven-pound bag of corn – and the next day Phyllis disappeared.

Fourteen

Charles said as it was nearing the end of December maybe she'd gone off to find a mate. She wouldn't have vanished as abruptly as that, I said – not when she'd been haunting us the way she had. We'd gone to town the previous afternoon. She'd been on the lawn when we left. Someone had undoubtedly spotted her, knew we were out, and had taken advantage of our absence.

I was pretty certain who it was, too. I looked meaningly at Fred Ferry when I saw him. I intended calling on *him* on Christmas morning and if the Ferrys were cooking pheasant...

Fred commented on her absence, too. Naturally he would, I thought. Part of his cover-up. Members of the moonlight fraternity are usually expert in the art of appearing innocent. I thought it a bit thick all the same when he asked where were thic li'l old bird then.

'Goin' to have her for thee Christmas dinner?' he said. 'I thought thee wussn't feein' her for nothin'.'

How could he, I thought – but just in case I was wrong I went clucking for her up the lane. Charles searched for her in the orchard – he'd been over there pruning trees a few days previously and had looked up to see her watching him from the nearby path as if she'd come along for company. If she did get broody, he said, that might well be where she'd build her nest, knowing it was our land and safe. She might already have decided on a spot and not be bothering to come down – obviously she'd get shyer as the mating season approached.

Not a sign. We'd said we wouldn't get fond of her but inevitably, of course, we had. Every time I went out of the door I missed her and wished that she would come back. What a wonderful present it would be if she came back on Christmas Day, I thought, as the short winter days went by and the yard stayed silent and pheasant-less. She wouldn't, of course. Why Christmas Day, anyway? Pheasants didn't know about that. In any case she was probably hanging in Fred Ferry's larder, awaiting her Christmas Day appearance on his table...

Believe it or not, she did come back on Christmas Day. We were expecting friends and I'd got up early to put the turkey on and gone out to change the cats' boxes – and there she was, padding quietly about in the vegetable garden as if she'd never been away.

Six days' solid absence. We couldn't think where she could have been. Certainly she couldn't have been thinking of nesting, she was so obviously back to stay. She followed me down the garden, looking for her corn and stayed

outside the kitchen door all day. We fed her with tit-bits till they practically came out of her ears and the cats sat in the window and watched her. On the lawn – it was Christmas, so never mind if she dug holes – Annabel ate apples and carrots and Christmas pudding and complacently watched her too.

'Din' eat her then?' Fred Ferry shouted across, going past in the afternoon. He had a sprig of holly in his cap but why he had his knapsack on his shoulder on Christmas Day... Charles said he probably picked it up automatically and didn't feel right without it – just as whatever day it was he had to have his tramp around the hills. Maybe, I said. Personally I doubted it... Then I remembered how wrong I'd been in suspecting him over Phyllis.

'Happy Christmas!' I called after him up the hill. Poor Fred. He nearly fell flat in his tracks.

I was wrong, though, when I said now we were a complete unit again – ourselves, Annabel, the cats and Phyllis. A few days later an enormous cock-pheasant appeared – the most gorgeous we'd ever seen – and started strutting grandly with the little hen on the hillside behind the cottage. He wouldn't venture into the yard, though. When we threw out food and Phyllis came flapping down, he stayed where he was looking anxious.

So that was where she'd been during those six missing days, we said. Up in the forest courting. She'd certainly picked herself a handsome husband and we were immensely flattered that she'd brought him back. Whether they'd stay together for nesting... we didn't know much about pheasants' habits; there is very little about them in bird books, but it would be nice, we thought, if they did.

We imagined them bringing the brood down to visit us. Philip, as we named him gracing our lawn. He was as beautiful at close quarters as any peacock. His metallic copper back merged through gold to a glossy green head, his front was gold spotted with black, his tail swept the ground like a train. He had scarlet wattles, two feathered tufts that stuck up on his head like ears... indeed he was a gorgeous fellow. Crossed with an exotic, probably, and how dowdy little Phyllis had managed to attract him... She'd probably told him about the corn, said Charles. And anyway, had I looked at Phyllis properly lately? I looked now. Goodness gracious, she'd grown still more even since Fred Ferry had commented on her – and *her* coat was beautiful too. Probably the result of the way we'd been feeding her. Phyllis had changed from a woebegone waif into a most desirable young pheasant lady.

Even so, she was still smaller than the next pheasant she introduced, another hen, whom Charles named Maisie. It looked as if she intended to come on the strength too, he said, so we might as well call her something.

Either pheasant hens are more trusting than the cocks, or they are more placid during the courting season. At any rate, although Maisie was never as tame as Phyllis – she retreated warily when we got too near her and would never look directly at us, while Phyllis appeared to have a system of pre-determining our moves by staring up at us straight in the eye – she did, from the moment she appeared, come in and feed in the yard, which was more then could be said for Philip, who strutted, beautiful as a Fabergé weathercock, worriedly up on the hill taking care to keep his distance.

Were Phyllis and Maisie his harem? we wondered. But no, there was one more to come. Seeing Maisie wandering round the yard on her own one afternoon (Phyllis's presence wasn't quite so continuous these days), I gave her some corn and, after I had come back indoors, heard a most peculiar bubbling sound. It wasn't the ordinary pheasant clucking so, wondering if perhaps she wasn't feeling so good, I went to watch her through the window. Sass, of course, was already there. He spent most of his time these days silently regarding pheasants out of windows with what was supposed to be sinister intent, but the pheasants didn't take any notice of him.

'She's calling a cock-bird,' said Charles, coming to watch over my shoulder. Philip, I thought... The old, old story... She was trying to steal him from Phyllis while Phyllis was out of the way. At that moment, sure enough, a cock-pheasant came over the wall, but it wasn't the handsome Philip. This one was buff-coloured, smaller, and had lost his tail somewhere – probably a fox had grabbed at it. He hardly looked the mate for the attractive Maisie, any more than one would have expected Philip to have fallen for Phyllis. But there he was – Charles immediately named him Maurice – pecking bashfully at the corn with her in the yard. Sass looked menacingly at them out of the window, but love was obviously oblivious of all.

Seeing that Maurice came to no harm, within a day or two Philip fluttered down from the hillside as well. We now had a quartet who seemed to have adopted us. It was going to be interesting to see how things developed. Meanwhile – by this time Christmas was a fortnight behind us – another strange story was in the making.

There was an elderly widow, whom I will call Mrs Laye, who lived some twelve miles away from us. She liked painting and we had met her through an art exhibition Charles had organised some while before, when she told me she had read my books. She had two cats – Belinda, a long-haired tabby and Franz, a Seal-point Siamese. She had asked us to tea to see them. We liked Mrs Laye and so we had gone. Belinda was elderly and gentle. Franz was two years old, intelligent and like quicksilver. This was a good while before we had Sass, but when we did, one thing that struck me immediately was how much he resembled Franz. Not just in looks, though they had the same pointed face and gangling, waif-like body. Franz, too, carried things around in his mouth and haunted his Mum like a shadow.

He was a friendly cat, but scared of men, since he rarely ever met any. The one exception was a Franciscan monk attached to the local Catholic Church, whose special task was visiting the elderly and who often came to tea with Mrs Laye. Father Francis – Franz was named after him – was our fellow guest when we were there. He was a jovial, bearded giant of a man who had formerly been a probation officer. My most striking memory of that afternoon – it was winter and very cold – was of Father Francis sitting in an armchair by the fire wearing enormous open sandals – without socks, which made me shiver – carefully supporting, in the lap of his brown woollen habit, one blissfully warm Siamese.

Mrs Laye wrote to me regularly after that and I invited her to come and see the gang. She was reticent about imposing, as she called it, but had come the previous summer. A friend had brought her over, as she didn't own a car. She so enjoyed her afternoon. She sat for ages with Sass on

her lap, commenting on his likeness to Franz. She had her photograph taken with him. She loved Shebalu, she loved Annabel, she loved the cottage – but it was Sass who made her day. She'd brought him a ball that bounced particularly high – Franz had one, she said – and when he obligingly brought it back to her and put it at her feet, Mrs Laye's happiness was complete.

I remembered it all so vividly when, two weeks after Christmas, the friend who'd brought her over rang to say that Mrs Laye was dead.

I was stunned. I'd had a letter from her just before Christmas telling me all she was doing – practising for carol-singing with a party from the church, helping at a Christmas bazaar, organising an old people's social, Father Francis had been to tea... She'd had to put her Christmas tree in the hall because Franz kept taking off the decorations. He particularly liked walking around carrying a little glass bell in his mouth – he loved to hear it tinkle. She finished by saying she was looking forward to our visiting her in the New Year. How glad I was now that I'd said we would.

She'd been found sitting in her armchair in front of the fireplace. It was a peaceful way for her to go. The thing that upset me most, that freezing January day, was to hear that Franz was missing.

Someone had noticed that Mrs Laye hadn't taken in her milk and a neighbour had gone in through the back way. Naturally his first concern had been for her. He hadn't given a thought to the cats – who, said her friend, were never let out on their own so they must have been in there with her. They must have been cold and hungry. She had been dead two days when she was found and the cats had

never missed a meal in their lives. They would have been frightened, too, by someone suddenly coming in; they would probably have hidden somewhere.

In the confusion that followed Belinda must have slipped out through the door – she'd been found sitting on the doorstep that evening and was being looked after by an elderly couple whose dog had just died and who were absolutely delighted to have her. But Franz, so intelligent, so full of zest when he was on his own with Mrs Laye but so nervous in the presence of strangers – especially men, and there had been police and a doctor and ambulance men trampling through the house – Franz had completely disappeared.

What could they do? asked Mrs Laye's friend. If she liked, Charles and I would come over and help search for him, I said, but as he was such a nervous cat, it would be better for neighbours who knew him better to call him – and put food down for him and watch for his return. Most likely he'd come back like Belinda – and if there was any question of finding a home for him when he did, we'd do our best to find him a good one and look after him in the interim.

We waited for news. Three days later one of Mrs Laye's neighbours phoned me. There was still no sign of Franz, she said. She didn't think he'd run out like Belinda, though – he was too nervous. She was sure he was still inside the house. She'd searched for him herself as soon as she'd heard the news – the police had given her permission. The first place she'd looked had been Mrs Laye's bed, knowing that Franz always slept with her and that that was where he went when strangers came and he was scared. There had been no trace of him anywhere. Another neighbour had searched

later, and so had the police. But she still had a feeling that he *was* in there somewhere, and now he'd been without food for almost a week. Mrs Laye's next of kin was a cousin, but she didn't know her name or where she lived. Mrs Laye had talked about me so much. Could I do anything? I'd do what I could, I said, and I rang the police.

It was late on a Saturday night, but they were most co-operative. I asked if it was possible for Charles and me to go to the house with them and put food and water down. If there was a cat in there it must be starving, and it didn't bear thinking about.

They'd searched the house twice for the cat already, said the sergeant, but if I thought it might still be there... They couldn't let me in themselves. The keys had been handed to Mrs Laye's solicitor who couldn't be contacted till Monday morning. But things were quiet at the station. He'd send a constable round right away to look through the windows with a torch and if he did see a cat he'd let me know.

I thanked him. How could I explain to someone who didn't know cats that even if Franz *were* starving he wouldn't sit in the middle of a room while somebody shone a torch on him? His instinct would be to hide. I wondered all the same why, if Franz were in the house, he hadn't been seen at a window. Our two would have been bawling for help long ago.

First thing on Monday morning I rang the solicitor, who arranged to meet Charles and me at the house at two o'clock. He had several appointments that day and after lunch was the earliest he could manage. I was on tenterhooks all morning. If Franz was still in there he must be so hungry. By now it was more than a week.

When we met the solicitor there was another delay. He didn't have the keys. He'd left them, he said, with a local shopkeeper – there was only one set and police and relatives had had to go in and that seemed to be the simplest solution. He'd just called to fetch them, but the shopkeeper was out. It was his half-day and he'd gone to town, and wouldn't be back until five o'clock. If we'd like to come back then...

If we'd gone round the house with the solicitor it might have been different. I would have left food and water as I'd intended. But he had another appointment – the shopkeeper would go round with us, he said. Perhaps we'd let him know if we found the cat.

The shopkeeper, when he returned, was tired and cold, and he too knew very little about cats. All this fuss, he said... He and a policeman had searched the house twice – even moved out furniture and looked. The cat wasn't there. He'd bet us a thousand pounds we wouldn't find it. Just because the neighbours had got this idea... However, to satisfy us and as the solicitor had said we could, he'd get the keys and take us round.

We looked in every room and peered up the chimneys, though there was no sign of soot in the fireplaces. Under and behind furniture. Charles turned armchairs upside down. Under beds. Charles got down and peered up into the springs. He wouldn't be *there*, I said. In each room the shopkeeper stood and watched us, sighing exasperatedly and rattling the keys. He closed each door as we came out. When I suggested leaving the food and water he said there'd been untouched food in the kitchen when he'd first come in – he'd had to throw it away because it was smelling. There was no point in our putting more down.

The funeral was the next day. Friends and relatives would be coming there afterwards – they would only throw it out. He couldn't leave the doors open, either. This was how he'd found them. Shut.

We parted from him on the pavement, he understandably irritated at what he considered our interference. As he'd predicted, we hadn't found the cat. I was sure myself now that Franz couldn't be in there. For one thing there hadn't been any smell, which one would certainly have expected if a cat had been locked for a week in an empty house. I could only think, now, that Franz *had* run out and had found himself a home somewhere else. Maybe someone had taken him in who didn't want to part with him and was keeping quiet about his turning up.

I hoped that was so. I couldn't get out of my mind Mrs Laye's account of Franz walking round carrying the bell off the Christmas tree. Only a few weeks ago he'd been sheltered, loved, and had never known what it was to be cold or hungry. Now where was he? I shivered in the icy night. Please... Not lost, like Seeley...

I wish I'd taken the shopkeeper up on his bet. The RSPCA would have been a thousand pounds richer. A fortnight later – three weeks after Mrs Laye's death – Franz was at last discovered.

He was in Mrs Laye's bed. He couldn't have been there all the time – it was the first place the neighbour had looked in and she assured me that she had opened it right up, knowing it to be his favourite refuge. But three weeks later Mrs Laye's cousin and the friend who lived with her, a retired nurse, had been packing a suitcase with some of her belongings on the bed. They'd been doing it

gradually in the fortnight since the funeral and had been at the house quite regularly. They, too, had looked for Franz every time they went there and had been certain he wasn't there. They had packed several cases on the bed during that time and would certainly have noticed any disturbance. Nevertheless, that particular afternoon they noticed a bump in the bed, pulled back the bed-clothes and there he was. All there seemed to be of him, said Mrs Laye's cousin's friend, the nurse, was a pair of numbed blue eyes.

He must have crawled there to die. They dropped everything and rushed him home. The Vet was away and couldn't come until next morning. Meanwhile the nurse gave him hot milk and took him to bed with her. In the middle of the night, she said, Franz – still only semi-conscious – suddenly wet her and the bed.

The Vet, when he came, thought that had possibly saved his life – through fear or cold he'd somehow retained his urine and that had prevented him from dehydrating. As it was, it was an absolute miracle that he had survived for three weeks without food or water. We'd been told, when Seeley was missing and we were searching for him everywhere, that a cat would die without water after a fortnight.

I got regular bulletins. Franz was taking chicken broth. Franz was now eating chicken. The Vet had said he was going to be all right, and his kidneys were quite undamanged. There was just one thing, said the nurse on the phone. They'd heard how anxious I'd been about him. They knew Mrs Laye had talked about me so much. Did I think perhaps I had a prior right to him? He was such a loving, gentle cat. They'd dearly love to keep him...

Goodness, I said, nearly sobbing down the phone. Who had more right to him than they did? His owner's cousin and her friend, who had found him and saved his life? I could only give thanks that they had done and kick myself for not insisting that night on leaving the doors of the rooms open and putting food and water down, so that Franz might have come out from his hiding place to have it.

He lives the life of Riley in Bristol now. He bosses Mrs Laye's cousin's cat, Jamie, around unmercifully and has completely taken over the household. He likes chicken and carrying things round in his mouth and is the image of Sass. Mrs Laye, I know, would be happy for him. I hope she would think, too, that Charles and I did our best – though I shall always feel sick at the thought that we'd gone into the house where he must have been all the time and had been unable to find him.

Fifteen

It was a long while before I could think of Franz without turning cold at the thought of his ordeal. But life goes on, bringing humour as well as sadness and, while it was still winter, Dora and Nita came to supper and we had a little light relief.

They arrived in a gale. They always arrive spectacularly. Once they came when it was snowing. Another time the stream was on the verge of flooding and they had to paddle up the path. This time it was a gale and they were practically swept into the cottage – where, the fire having been perfectly all right until half an hour before, smoke was now billowing in big black clouds out of the chimney and rolling relentless around the room.

When it does this, it is always when we have visitors. I remember it happening once when some people were coming to see the cats and I'd lit the fire to set the rural

background. It set the background all right. One shouldn't open a window to let smoke out – it only draws more down – but if you only have one reception room and you can't see across it and the air is filled with floating smuts... one *must* open the windows, said Charles, opening all three of them, whereupon the smoke poured lustily out.

At that moment the visitors arrived. They got out of the car and just stared. It must have looked odd – smoke pouring out of all three front windows like a Mississippi steamboat and Charles waving a welcome to them through the smog. Even more odd when they came inside. Because of the open windows it was like the Arctic and another lot of smoke had just belched down, and the cats were on their stomachs under the table with their ears down flatly refusing to come out. The visitors didn't stay long, which was a pity, because half an hour later the wind had dropped. It didn't drop the night Dora and Nita came to supper, however. It darned well stayed with us all night.

We put up with the smoke at first. Dora and Nita are very resourceful – both were Guide Captains for years. When I apologised they said not to worry – don't forget they were used to camp fires. The thing to do was to get *below* the smoke, because it rises. Suiting their action to the words, the pair of them lay down on the hearthrug, Charles stood opening the window in short bursts and I, holding on to the cats to stop them diving through it, wondered why it always had to happen to us.

Eventually it became obvious that the gale wasn't going to abate and that the only thing to do was to let the fire down. Charles said right-ho, he'd just fetch the electric one – at which point the lights went out. This is another favourite

happening when we have gales or visitors – our electricity comes by overhead cable and if it isn't that the wind has brought the wire down or lightning struck the transformer, somebody has probably been reversing outside in the lane and knocked down the pole with their car.

In this case it was the cable down and the electricity was off all night. Fortunately we were having a cold supper. We ate it by candlelight, warmed bleakly by a paraffin stove, while I tried to boil a saucepan of water for coffee on what was left of the fire. There wasn't much, but what there was made the water taste of smoke. I made the coffee. We sat there drinking it – Dora and Nita, of course, were by this time upright. I just happened to look across at our big oak table, on which I'd placed lighted candles in candelabra – a present from Elizabeth Linington, an American writer, which goes most effectively with our decor – and there was Sass, just about to touch one of the candles with his stretched out nose.

I yelled. He jumped. So did everybody else.

'He's burnt himself,' said Charles. Nonsense, I said; he wouldn't be so stupid. But he jolly well had. For weeks he had a pink scar on his nose where he'd put it against the candle.

What was more, our friends were going to a party the following night. They had to wash their hair next morning to get the smell of the smoke out. Dora, wanting to wear the same long tartan skirt, said she'd hung it out on the line for hours but it had still reeked of smoke. She'd hopefully sprayed it with air-freshener, but it hadn't really helped. She'd had to explain to the people she sat next to about having come to supper with us. Funny, she said. She only

had to mention our names and the other people said 'Say no more.'

I wonder sometimes whether having Siamese cats creates the atmosphere for untoward happenings, even when the cats are only remotely involved, or whether it is that people prone to such occurrences inevitably become the owners of Siamese cats.

Take, for instance, my friend who had the Siamese that got roaring drunk on sherry. When she bought her first Siamese kitten there were no such things as plastic bowls and the breeder told her to get a large enamel pie-dish or roasting tin to serve as an earthbox. She went to the hardware shop. The man showed her two sizes of dishes. No, she shook her head; those were too small. Halfway up the ladder to where there were some more stores on a high self he called down 'Is it for a turkey?'

'No,' she called back, 'for a cat.' The shop was full of customers. Mia is Swiss by birth. She said that though eventually somebody began to laugh, for a moment all those English people looked at her in stunned silence, obviously wondering whether it was right about foreigners eating cats.

Take, again, the story of a Tabby Point Siamese called Oliver, who belongs to a friend of mine in Oxford. Oliver developed rhinitis and the Vet prescribed a disposable plastic syringe, graduated into six doses, with which Marjorie had to put medicine into his mouth. By the time it got to the third dose, Oliver had had enough. He bit the business end off the syringe and swallowed it.

Panic-stricken, Marjorie rushed him to the Vet who laughed till she cried when she heard the story. She said the

syringe end would probably pass right through and do no harm but in case there was any trouble, here was another syringe containing liquid paraffin and if necessary Marjorie should give him one dose. Marjorie said she came away with a dismal picture of his biting off that one, too, and starting an endless cycle of swallowed syringe ends. Fortunately, however, the first end reappeared and she didn't have to give him the paraffin... Which is but one small incident in the life of a sober Doctor of Literature who is owned by a Siamese.

Take, once more – just to show it isn't only in England that people are ruled by their cats – a story told me by Elizabeth Linington of what happened to some friends of hers one Christmas. She lives in California, they live in a small town halfway across America. Ringing them in mid-December she heard a woeful story of how Christmas was going to be a disaster because all the local supermarkets were out of a certain brand of turkey cat-food which was the only kind their ten-year-old cat would eat. He'd gone on strike and they had visions of him starving. The supermarkets wouldn't be having fresh supplies in until the New Year. How could they have a happy Christmas?

Elizabeth went to her own supermarket in California. They had the turkey cat-food there all right. She bought two cases and despatched them by air – there is an internal airmail service in America. She phoned other friends who lived nearer the couple and got them to send consignments as well, in case hers didn't get through as it was so near Christmas and there might be a delay in the mail.

On Christmas Eve she rang them again, certain that by this time the cat-food would have reached them and there'd

be two happy people and one contented cat blissfully awaiting Christmas. The cat was contented. The food had got through. It was the husband, Wilbur, who answered the phone. Cathy had her leg in plaster, he said. She'd broken every bone in her ankle and it wouldn't be right for months. It had had to be set under general anaesthetic... What? No, she hadn't slipped on the ice. She'd gone to open a tin of the turkey cat-food and had fallen over the cat.

Elizabeth herself has two Siamese and thereby hangs another tale. When I first knew her she lived in Los Angeles and owned a Havana and a Burmese cat. Fergus and Robin were quite a handful and one or other of them was always giving her a fright by staying out. She sat up the whole of one night, I remember, waiting for Fergus to come home, passing the time by writing me a detailed account of what was going on. The times at which she went out to call him, the places she searched, including the lonely nearby schoolyard at midnight...

Elizabeth writes detective stories under her own name and also as Dell Shannon and Lesley Egan. Anyone who has read them can imagine what her report was like. It would have done credit to her famous detective, Luis Mendoza. At 8.30 in the morning Fergus returned, the case was closed and Elizabeth mailed the full report to me. There was another occasion when Robin was ill and the competent, no-nonsense crime writer, who was at that time in the middle of a book, lay for hours on the floor feeding him with raw steak under her bed, that being the only place where he would eat. They certainly were a handful. I'm sure she didn't believe it when I told her they weren't nearly as bad as Siamese.

In due course Fergus and Robin died. Elizabeth wrote that she was getting a dog – one she could exercise on a lead. It would be a good thing to have a guard-dog in times that were growing so troublesome and she wouldn't have to be always hunting, heart in mouth, for absent cats.

She acquired Star, a Keeshond, who carried her feeding bowl round in her mouth and barked fiercely on the recorder tapes Elizabeth sent me. It didn't seem right for her not to have cats, though, and when she moved two hundred miles north to Arroyo Grande – to a bungalow with an acre of ground for Star to roam in, which she enclosed with a high wire fence – it wasn't long before she was talking of getting a couple of kittens, now that she had a safe place.

She spoke of getting a couple of unwanted ones from the stray animals' pound in town. She was going in next day. Guess what? she enquired the next time I had a tape from her. She'd just got two Siamese! She'd heard of this breeder, she'd just called to have a look at them, she'd come home with Penelope and Pandora... Much as I was pleased to hear she'd got Siamese, which I always felt would be Elizabeth, I nearly had a fit when I thought of them in her new house which from the photographs she sent was quite magnificent.

The beautiful kitchen and dining-room; the antique chairs upholstered in white velvet; others in champagne-striped satin; the champagne carpet (Star has small feet); the long blue velvet curtains in her bedroom. She'd really gone to town in planning it all, and now she'd introduced Siamese cats!

Actually she seems to have achieved miracles. The velvet chairs still appear in photographs. Goodness knows how

she's preserved them since there are invariably two cats sitting smugly on them looking as though they've owned them for years. But the kitchen soon had to be partitioned off with transparent amber panels; people who design open kitchens don't know about Siamese cats. Three cat-trees now appear in the photographs, too, of a type which could only be found in America. Not a log nailed to a board and wrapped round with a piece of carpet such as we have for Sass and Shebalu. These consist of a series of shaggy-covered platforms like miniature diving-boards, alternating up a centre pole which is almost the height of the room and which grips the ceiling by means of a chromium tube containing a spring so that cats going up it can't knock it down.

There is a royal blue cat-tree in Elizabeth's bedroom, two amber ones on the porch... Originally the patio, it was cased in to make a porch where Penny and Pandora could play in safety, Elizabeth having visions of their otherwise scooting across the acre of garden and climbing the fence if they got the chance.

Rattan screens covered the window apertures... The cats didn't go *through* them? I thought when I heard it. Sure enough, on her next tape Elizabeth said she'd been on the phone one day and had seen a Siamese looking in at her through the study window. Fancy, she thought idly... those new neighbours must have a Siamese too... and then she suddenly realised she was looking at Pandora. She called a builder to put in permanent windows immediately, which turned the porch into a proper room, and now of course it has had to be rated, all on account of the cats...

After that it had to be furnished – and that is only *indoors*. Outside, Elizabeth now has two sheep: a ewe

called Marlene and a ram named Nicodemus whom she borrowed temporarily to keep down the grass and who, when she heard they were destined for the butcher, she naturally bought and added to the strength seeing that she has all that land. She has gophers, too, who spend their time undermining her rose-trees. Like us, she wouldn't dream of putting down poison. So she keeps buying new rose-trees, getting chased by Nicodemus, her problems with her lawn-mower would fill a book...

Just like us. As I tell her, and now I think she believes it – it *happens* when you take on Siamese cats.

Sixteen

With us, back in the Valley, spring and the caravanning season were approaching. The pheasants had left us by this time, but we weren't worrying so much about them now. First Phyllis and Maisie had stopped coming; presumably they were building their nests. For a week or two longer Philip and Maurice continued to appear on the lawn – never with the confidence that the hens had had, never coming close to the house, but obviously taking advantage of their girlfriends' absence to get what was going in the way of corn.

Then they too vanished – to look after the nests, I thought, until I looked it up in the bird book and discovered that they aren't that sort of bird at all. Only the hens sit on the eggs, which are laid in scanty nests in bracken or tall grass. Over in our orchard seemed a likely place, but if they were there, we never saw them.

According to the bird book pheasants are polygamous, which was another let-down to the idyll. I'd imagined Philip guarding Phyllis's nest, Maurice patrolling Maisie's, the four of them bringing their families to the garden in due course. It now seemed more likely that, the hens being occupied with their eggs, the two Don Juans had gone in search of other conquests. They could even have been philandering with other hens while courting Phyllis and Maisie. So much for romance in the pheasant world. As Shakespeare said, it was ever thus.

Tim Bannett had two goats by this time – Polly and a Toggenberg called Tanya. Both were in kid and he went past with them every day en route to his field up the lane. They weren't on leads. They followed him from affection as he'd hoped, pausing to nibble at top speed in the hedge then galloping like mad to catch him up. Eventually Polly produced three kids and Tanya had two and, until he sold the youngsters, he went past looking like a character from a frieze on an Arcadian vase, with seven of them skipping around him.

We loved to see it. The kids went up and down as if they were on springs and butted and chased each other like tiny clowns. Goats aren't everybody's pigeon, however. Back when they only had Polly, Liz had once called on Mrs Ferry while taking her for a walk and while they were talking Polly had gone into the house.

'She didn't do any damage,' Liz said later. 'She left some droppings on the carpet but, as I said to Mrs Ferry, they're all right so long as you don't step on them.' It was a new carpet. Mrs Ferry, practically incoherent, told me later that the droppings had rattled down on it like machine-gun

bullets. When there were seven of them she kept the broom handy and watched with an extremely jaundiced eye when they went by. As for Fred Ferry, by way of adding interest to local life, he and Miss Wellington weren't speaking.

It had started when Miss Wellington heard he was renting a piece of land behind her cottage. The old-style villager often does this – rents an odd bit of land that someone isn't using and raises extra crops of vegetables on it to sell. Fred, piqued perhaps by Tim's getting the use of the graveyard, had decided to go in for growing cabbages on a large scale and show everybody what was what. He'd accordingly rented the piece of land and, while he was putting in the plants the previous autumn, Miss Wellington had come out to object. She'd be able to smell them when she was in the garden, she said, and they looked so unsightly in the winter.

Fred, breathing something which could only be represented by asterisks, asked what about thic cabbages in the graveyard then? Miss Wellington said she couldn't see those because of the wall and anyway there was only one row of them.

Fred continued planting. That was that. A week or so later, when the leaves began to fall, Miss Wellington appeared, broom in hand, sweeping the lane outside the Ferrys' gate. Fred has a rather large sycamore which drops its leaves in the lane and in the normal course of things they stay there until the wind blows them away. Miss Wellington always predicts somebody will slip on them, of course, but nobody takes any notice. Now she was out sweeping them up herself.

'They're not *my* leaves,' she announced to nobody in particular when Fred came clumping down the path.

'Tain't thy lane either,' said Fred serenely, heading for the Rose and Crown.

One result of this little contretemps was that she didn't worry about the graveyard wall collapsing on him that winter. It wouldn't have done anyway, since Tim had cemented it, but that hadn't prevented her from worrying previously. 'Remember the dyke that nearly gave way in Holland?' she asked me once. 'And the little boy saved it by putting his hand in?' I did vaguely remember reading it in an infant primer when I was at school, though I'd completely forgotten it till she mentioned it. Not so Miss Wellington, who presumably saw herself saving Fred's life by rushing out and holding a stone up. Not any more, though. Not since the cabbages. At pub turning-out time her door remained firmly shut, much to the relief of the ungrateful Fred who said her shining thic torch at him gived he the willies.

Now it was spring, he was cutting his cabbages and Miss Wellington was complaining about that. Always lurking in that field, she said. She was sure he was up to no good. Quite a few people thought that when he went past with his knapsack, but – poor Fred – not when he was innocently cutting cabbages! Meanwhile, down at the cottage, our own thoughts were turning towards the caravan.

It had been quite a progressive winter. Charles had at last finished the dresser and very good indeed it looked with its gleaming pine panelling, red-tiled top and a set of matching cupboards above it. We'd decided against open shelves, realising that the only things likely to be on them for long would be two Siamese cats. As it was they sat on the dresser top convinced that it had been built specially for them to watch me. Charles said he hoped I didn't roll

pastry up there; he wouldn't fancy any if I did. Not after the muddy footprints I was forever wiping off it. I didn't. I am particular too.

Yet what happened when I *wanted* their footprints? Somebody had asked for their autographs and, seeing them lying peacefully together in front of the fire, I thought that if I dabbed a paw each with damp kitchen paper right at that moment, and plonked them on a card, that way I'd get their paw-prints before they realised it and we wouldn't have howls about how I was Murdering Them.

I dabbed. I plonked. Not the faintest smudge came off. I dabbed and plonked again. I had to go out, get mud and *put* it on their paws before I could get even the slightest impression. When I think of the letters they march over... the magazines people lend us... Income Tax returns... and there they were looking at me as if I'd gone out of my mind. Putting Dirt on their Paws, they said, pulling them away in horror, sniffing at them and fastidiously licking them. As I say a dozen times in the course of a day, with Siamese you never can win.

Anyway, the dresser was finished and the conservatory was coming along; people had stopped asking whether it was going up or down and the Rector was beginning to eye it with interest, obviously with the thought of grapes for the Harvest Festival in mind. The next job, said Charles, was to get the caravan out and go over it, and at the beginning of April we did. We hauled it up into the field, Charles checked the wheels and the brakes and the towing mechanism, I spring-cleaned the inside – and discovered, in so doing, where Lancelot had been that winter. Snug as a bug in the caravan – in the cupboard under the sink.

It must have been him. He hadn't appeared in the porch at all that winter. We'd wondered if he was dead. It could have been him that Sass had jumped on and flattened in the garden the previous summer and had eaten and as a result got worms... Anyway, I knew now it couldn't have been Lancelot. We'd been advised to put wire gauze around the rubber waste-pipe from the sink, where it goes through a hole in the caravan floor – otherwise, the man who'd sold us the van had told us, mice would get up there like one o'clock. We hadn't been able to obtain wire gauze. It seemed to have gone off the market. I cut a hole in a plastic yeast-tin cover instead, and fitted that round the pipe and put a stone on one edge to weight it down, and the first winter no mice had got in.

Undoubtedly because the previous owner had cleaned it out so well before he delivered it to us. So, I thought the second winter, had I. I'd left a packet of paper napkins in a drawer, an empty bag or two in the cupboard, thinking they'd come in handy the following year. Certainly nothing smelling of food, though. Just a half-used tablet of soap in a holder and a couple of candles for emergency use.

That had been enough. A mouse had chewed a hole through the plastic cover – presumably clinging to the pipe to do it. He'd made a nest in the paper napkins, eaten the paper bags, plus the candles and the soap, which he'd chewed level with the top of the holder. It was scented soap. Ugh, I thought. Lancelot certainly had peculiar taste... Why was I so certain it was him? Because the caravan was a considerable distance from the orchard and Charles's nut trees, but it will be remembered how Lancelot liked nuts, and around his nest in the drawer, where he could eat them

while in bed (the soap and candles had no doubt constituted reserve rations) were hundreds and hundreds of nutshells undoubtedly from Charles's best Kent Cobs.

I cleared it all out. Lancelot had obviously long since vacated the drawer and was probably living it up in the garden for the summer – telling all the other mice he met, no doubt, about how he owned his own caravan. Next winter, I said, there'd be wire gauze over that hole if I jolly well had to knit it myself. Now, though, we were back to the problem – were we going to take the cats?

Seventeen

Definitely not on our first trip of the year at any rate. We had decided to take the caravan to London – a proposal which, when we mentioned it to our neighbours, caused them considerable alarm.

'Never heard of nobody taking a caravan up there,' said Father Adams. 'Wheres't be goin' to put it? In Hyde Park?' Fred Ferry said he wouldn't like to be us with thic thing in all thic traffic. Charles told him we weren't going to be. We were going to the Caravan Club Harbour at Crystal Palace – on a Saturday afternoon around teatime, when there wouldn't be much traffic about. According to the instructions we came off the M4 at Exit 2, made for Chiswick, got on the South Circular Road, stuck to it until we came to the junction of Thurlow Park and South Croxted Road, then followed the directions in the handbook.

'Sounds all right', Ern Biggs said bluntly. 'But theest know what thee bist like. Whass thee goin' to do if theest get lost?'

Impossible, we said firmly. Not if we followed the South Circular signs. To our more appreciative friends we explained that we were taking the caravan up because hotels are now so terribly expensive and we intended to stay for ten days – to see the museums and art galleries and so on we'd never got round to, though we'd been meaning to visit them for years. We had a caravan that was home from home, so why pay steep hotel bills and probably not be able to sleep into the bargain? At Crystal Palace they had showers and hot water and telephones and the caravans stood on hard ground. There was a stop right opposite the entrance from which buses went to all parts of London – it was more convenient, even, than many hotels. What a marvellous idea, said caravanning friends who'd never thought of doing it themselves. They'd be interested to hear how we got on.

The fact was, people didn't have enough initiative, said Charles as we drove up the motorway at the beginning of May. Staying in stuffed-shirt hotels wasn't our cup of tea if we could help it. If one *had* to go to London, this was the way.

It was, as far as Chiswick. We'd left the cats at Burrowbridge, got on the motorway at Bridgwater, driven up to Exit 2 in three hours... Unfortunately at Chiswick we got lost, as Ern had predicted. Having done a hundred and fifty miles in three hours flat, it took us two and a half to do the last nineteen.

All had gone well to start with. We'd found the South Circular Road and were following it as instructed when we

suddenly came to a diversion sign. We followed that. To the left. Across a couple of intersections. To the right. To the right again. *Somewhere* the diversion must have ended, but either the authorities had forgotten to signify it or somebody had moved the sign.

My memory of what followed is somewhat kaleidoscoped. I remember Charles parking the caravan round corners every few minutes while I nipped out and asked the way. I remember a West Indian bus driver who nearly dropped when he saw us pull in behind him at a bus stop and then, giving us directions which involved crossing the busy road ahead, driving his double-decker out into the traffic and holding it up for us while we sailed majestically across.

If we'd followed his directions to the letter we'd probably have been all right but we thought we'd gone wrong when we saw a sign saying 'To The West End'. It was evening by now. The Saturday evening traffic was heading theatrewards. I could see us ending up in Trafalgar Square. 'To think,' I said, 'only this morning we were in the Valley. What on earth are we doing here?'

'Looking for Crystal Palace,' Charles said determinedly as he turned off once more to the left.

We got there eventually, after various people had given us different instructions. To go via Hammersmith Bridge. To go via Richmond. One said not to go over any bridge at all. For the record, we went over just about every bridge along that stretch of the Thames. Kew Bridge we went over four times. I remember some people standing at the bus stop at the beginning of it looking at us idly when we went past them the first time and staring at us as if they were seeing things when we came back. They were, of course. Realising

we'd made a mistake we'd circled briskly to the left and were trundling back over again.

'Not back the way we *came*!' I said warningly as we reached the other side. Charles obediently turned off to the right, circled round the back streets, came out heading for the bridge once more... Unfortunately turning to the right, where we should have gone, was forbidden from that direction, so we had to go over it again. Didn't it remind him of the time we went round Edmonton in circles in the camper? I asked. Charles said he was too busy to be reminded of anything.

We got there in the end. I wanted to give up and drive back to Somerset at one point but Charles said no, we must carry on. I felt as if we'd done a two-man expedition to Katmandu by the time we turned in at the Caravan Harbour gates. Not that we were the only ones to get lost, of course. According to the warden most people do. We met one man there who'd towed a caravan from Greece. He'd had no trouble at all, he said – right across Europe, through Yugoslavia, Germany, Holland, driving on the wrong side of the road up from Harwich – but he'd spent two solid hours, once he had the Crystal Palace television mast in his sights, trying to get to it round one-way streets.

We spent a marvellous ten days sightseeing and even then we didn't take in everything. We must come up and do it again, said Charles as, sated with art galleries, museums, Oxford Street and getting lost in Hampton Court Maze, we bowled triumphantly back down the motorway to Somerset. (This time we'd got from Crystal Palace to the M4 in thirty-five minutes and Charles was feeling pleased with the outfit.) Super, I said. The caravan's potential was

terrific. But I *would* like a holiday with the cats. That, after all, was why we'd bought it. When did he think we could try it out?

Soon, said Charles. In a few weeks' time. But still we kept delaying setting a definite date. Mainly because, every time we got round to considering it, something happened to put us off.

Take Sass and his worm, for instance. If you remember, he'd had one back in the autumn as the result of eating that mouse on the lawn. Pauline had noticed the signs when he and Shebalu were staying with her and, when I'd rung her to see how they were, had asked if she should give them each a tablet. If one cat had a worm, she said, the other would probably have one too, so she might as well dose them both at once.

She did. They'd come home full of beans, tearing around the cottage like racehorses. Sass in particular was all zip and sparkling eyes, his holiday and his worm tablet having done him good. So when, after we came back from London, he showed signs of having a worm again – obviously he'd caught a mouse we didn't know about – I rang Pauline, got the name of the tablets and obtained a couple from the Vet.

They had to be taken on an empty stomach. 'Give the tablets to them at mid-day,' said Pauline. 'That'll be a good three hours after their breakfast. You mustn't feed them for at least another three hours afterwards, so they'll be all right for their supper at five. That way they won't have to miss a meal. They make such a fuss if they have to go without.'

They do indeed, and what I hadn't the nerve to confess to her was that our two didn't have just the two meals a

day that adult Siamese should have. Ever since Louisa's cat Ginger came to stay and Sass had seen him eating his minced beef on the dot of twelve, he, too, had demanded food at mid-day and, to keep him happy, he'd got it. Shebalu too, because I couldn't feed one without the other, though she didn't worry so much. It was Sass who always reminded me. Dead on twelve-thirty, if I was working upstairs in the study, I'd hear the sitting-room door creak and he'd come up and demand to be let in. He'd then stand on my lap with his head under my chin so I couldn't possibly type and was bound to hear his stomach rumbling. I *had* to give him a spoonful or two. It would have been like *Oliver Twist* if I didn't.

How, then, to give him his tapeworm tablet? *Hamlet* wouldn't be in it if he missed his mid-day snack. The answer – and never have Charles and I felt nobler – was for us to get up at five in the morning. We went downstairs, lifted Sass from their chair, and Charles held him on the table while I put the tablet in his mouth. I'd lain awake most of the night anticipating that moment. Supposing we couldn't get him to swallow it? What did we do then? I needn't have worried. *Anything* Sass got in his mouth was there to be eaten. He didn't even stop purring while it went down.

Shebalu was more difficult. She squirmed frantically and tried to spit the tablet out, but I held her mouth and down it went. I felt quite triumphant when we were back in bed. How simple it had been, I said. I was so elated, I couldn't see a single obstacle to our taking them with us in the caravan. It was just a matter of being *determined* in our outlook, I said – not anticipating trouble at every turn.

I hadn't anticipated trouble as a result of giving Sass that worm tablet, but we got it just the same. We came down at eight, gave the cats their breakfast around nine – those horrible old worms were gone now, weren't they? I said. It was mid-morning when I noticed that, while Shebalu was asleep in front of the fire, there was no sign at all of Sass.

I rushed upstairs, downstairs, looked in all the cupboards – absolutely no sign of him anywhere. He must have got out, I thought – maybe he was up at Fred Ferry's after sherry. I was just about to rush up the hill to check when there was a hefty thump (I was going through the sitting-room at the time) as Sass descended from the topmost bookshelf. He never went up there during the day. He never went up there at all unless Shebalu dared him. Yet here he was now, obviously up there of his own accord, diving exuberantly down through the lampshade... belting round the room from the piano to the Welsh dresser, across to the bureau, up the back of the carved chairs... He tore round the cottage on and off all day while Shebalu watched him with her lorgnette look. (Always fully in control of herself is our blue girl. Even a worm tablet fails to affect her.) He was so full of beans that, while we were listening to the six o'clock news, he came hurdling over the low side-table where I'd put the radio. Wham! He slammed right into it, nearly knocked himself out, and it didn't improve the radio either.

Honestly, I said. When I thought of him in a caravan... Steady on now, said Charles. What had I been saying about not anticipating trouble? As a matter of fact, he'd had an idea. Why didn't we rehearse taking the cats away with us? We could camp out with them in the caravan while it was

still in our own field. Sleep up there with them at night. If they did get out there'd be no harm done – we were only on our own doorstep. But it would give us a chance to iron out any problems, then we could take them away with us with confidence.

Which was why a couple of days later, had anybody been watching, they could have seen us carrying up sleeping bags, saucepans, baskets of provisions and an earthbox and stowing them in the caravan. For just about the first time ever, however, nobody *was* watching. We'd chosen, quite by accident, a day when the contents of a house in the village were being auctioned and our regular passers-by – Father Adams, Fred Ferry, Ern Biggs and, since he bought his field, Tim Bannett – had all gone along to it hoping for bargains.

Thus it was that our movements went unrecorded and that when we were in the caravan that night (it was dusk and we'd drawn the curtains and lit our pressure oil-lamp to save carrying up the battery for electricity, and Charles was playing his recorder saying wasn't this great, and I was trying to prevent Sass from burning his nose on the lamp-glass) there was a bang on the door, a voice demanded who was in there, and we nearly shot out of our skins.

It was Tim. Coming back late from his field and seeing the light, he'd thought there were squatters in the van. We thanked him for his vigilance, explained what we were doing... even he, used as he was to us and non-conformist himself, looked shaken as he went on his way. Camping out with water containers and an oil-lamp, I could see him thinking, not a hundred yards from our own cottage...

His surprise was nothing to that which beset Fred Ferry at five o'clock next morning, however, when, hearing the

sound of footsteps moving round the caravan, I sat up, looked out of the window, and met him eyeball to eyeball peering in.

What he was doing around at that hour we didn't ask. His knapsack was on his shoulder as usual. And if it did occur to us to wonder, we kept our thoughts to ourselves. What he said – which could very well have been true, since the cats had been gawking out of the windows all night, marching consistently over Charles and me to get to them, which was why I was wide awake at five o'clock – was that he'd seen Sass looking out of a window and thought he'd got locked in.

'I knows what a tizzy theest get into if he was missing,' he explained. 'So I come over to have a look. By Gorry, it put years on I when I seen *thy* face at the window.'

It might have been better put, but we could appreciate how he felt. We explained to him why we were there. He said 'Oh ah,' but he seemed to be pondering about something as he went on his way up the hill.

We only spent a few nights in the caravan. Thanks to Fred, the news had got round. It was surprising how many people took to walking through the Valley in the evenings to see if what they'd heard was true. For years we'd had a reputation for being eccentric, but there didn't seem to be any point in making it worse. Besides, said Charles, we'd now proved we could sleep with them in the caravan. (We had? I thought. It was news to me!) It was coping during the day we had to practise.

We did. We practised practically every day for weeks, but we never got it to work. Take meals, for instance. The only way we could eat those with dignity was to shut the

cats in the car. To do it authentically, as we would if we were really caravanning, we had to park the car in the field alongside the van. We'd then have lunch, say, at the table in the caravan window, ducking when people we knew went past. Ducking wasn't much use, however, when riders were going by on horseback and could look down on us, and we heard some interesting theories as to what we were doing.

'Cracked,' said one. 'Have been for years.'

'Maybe they've got the decorators in the cottage,' suggested another.

'What are they doing crouched on the floor then?' asked a third. 'And why have they got their car in there with the cats bawling their heads off inside?'

'Like I said. Cracked,' said the first.

It was just as difficult when the cats were in the van. They opened cupboards, knocked things down, were forever trying to get out of one of the doors. Once I found Sass in the wardrobe, his long black hind legs just touching the ground, with his front claws hooked firmly above his head in one of Charles's anoraks, which had been left there from a previous holiday. As usual, when in distress, he was completely silent. Supposing he'd done that while we were away, I said. He could have been strung up there for hours and no one would have known. It just wasn't safe to leave him in a caravan, the way he could open doors.

Charles said he'd put a hook on it. He did. He put hooks on all the doors. The next thing I found Sass suspended from was the horizontal opening bar of the rooflight. I shut my eyes just for a moment one afternoon while I was keeping watch on the pair of them and when I opened them, there he was. Dangling by his front paws from the bar like

a trapeze artist. Silent as usual *in extremis*. Eyes round with apprehension. He must have tried to edge across from the top of the wardrobe and had slipped.

I rescued him. When I turned round, Shebalu was in the earthbox. That hadn't done her Nerves any good, she said. Her bottom began to rise at the thought of it. I dropped Sass and rushed to sit her down.

Which is why, as I finish this book, we still haven't taken the cats with us in the caravan, though we hope to do so any day now. Not for long holidays. For those they will go to Burrowbridge. But just for the odd weekend...

We had advertised for a quiet corner of an orchard or a field by the sea in Dorset, where we can be entirely on our own. Where cats swinging from curtain rods, or doing a tumble-drier act in the car at mealtimes won't attract undue attention.

Maybe if we do that we *could* take Annabel too, says Charles, the eternal optimist. She is *not* going to travel in the caravan, I tell him, even if he *could* construct a ramp. Perhaps we could get her a small-sized horse-box then, he suggested on one occasion. To hook on behind the caravan? I asked, visualising a procession like a Toy Town train. Of course not, he said. It wouldn't take long to run up and down a couple of times from the cottage to Dorset – first with the caravan, then with Annabel in a little box.

Annabel, in fact, likes it immensely at the Pursey's farm, where she bosses the cows and sheep around. Last time she was there they put her in with the sheep and the ram, and had a fit when he started to chase her. They needn't have worried. The two of them disappeared in a cloud of dust over the rise of the field. A few minutes later they came

thundering back. This time Annabel was in pursuit of the ram, who was going like the clappers. They had never seen him so quiet, they said, as he was for the rest of the holiday.

But the cats... we really do intend to take them one of these days. They are so much part of our lives. We bought the caravan because of them; it is our second home – and what is home without the comfort of cats?

CATS
IN THE BELFRY

'The most enchanting cat book ever'
Jilly Cooper

DOREEN TOVEY

CATS IN THE BELFRY

Doreen Tovey

£6.99   Paperback   ISBN: 978 1 84024 452 6

'It wasn't, we discovered as the months went by, that Sugieh was particularly wicked. It was just that she was a Siamese.'

Animal lover Doreen and her husband Charles acquire their first Siamese kitten to rid themselves of an invasion of mice. But Sugieh is not just any cat. She's an actress, a prima donna, an iron hand in a delicate, blue-pointed glove. She quickly establishes herself as queen of the house, causing chaos daily by screaming like a banshee, chewing up telegrams, and tearing holes in anything made of wool.

First published over forty years ago, this warm and witty classic tale is a truly enjoyable read for anyone who's ever been owned by a cat.

'If there is a funnier book about cats I for one do not want to read it. I would hurt myself laughing, might even die of laughter'
THE SCOTSMAN

'Every so often, there comes along a book – or if you're lucky books – which gladden the heart, cheer the soul… Just such books are those written by Doreen Tovey'   CAT WORLD

'A chaotic, hilarious and heart-wrenching love affair with this most characterful of feline breeds.'   THE PEOPLE'S FRIEND

CATS
IN MAY

From the bestselling author of
Cats In The Belfry

DOREEN TOVEY

CATS IN MAY

Doreen Tovey

£6.99   Paperback   ISBN: 978 1 84024 497 7

'All our animals showed their independence at a dishearteningly early age.'

The Toveys attempt to settle down to a quiet life in the country. Unfortunately for them, however, their tyrannical Siamese cats have other ideas.

From causing an uproar on the BBC to staying out all night and claiming to have been kidnapped, Sheba and Solomon's outrageous behaviour leaves the Toveys at their wits' end. Meanwhile Doreen has to contend with her husband's disastrous skills as a handyman, and a runaway tortoise called Tarzan.

Both human and animal characters come to life on the page, including Sidney the problem-prone gardener and Blondin the brandy-swilling squirrel. This witty and stylish tale will have animal-lovers giggling to the very last page.

'…will have animal lovers giggling to the very last page.'
YOUR CAT MAGAZINE

'No-one writes about cats with more wit, humour and affection than Doreen Tovey. Every word is a delight!'
THE PEOPLE'S FRIEND

THE
NEW BOY

From the bestselling author of *Cats In The Belfry*

DOREEN TOVEY

THE NEW BOY

Doreen Tovey

£6.99   Paperback   ISBN: 978 1 84024 517 2

'So there we were, driving along with an earth-box, a bag of turkey and, squalling his head off on my knee in Sheba's basket, the new boy.'

The Toveys are no strangers to disaster, particularly the Siamese-related kind, but when their beloved Solomon dies unexpectedly, they're faced with a completely new type of problem – do they find another cat to replace the one they've lost?

The animals always win in the Tovey household and this time is no exception. It is with the interests of Solomon's (very audibly) grieving sister Sheba at heart that Doreen and Charles set off in search of Solomon Secundus, affectionately known as Seeley.

Joined by a myriad of endearing characters, Seeley ensures he's living up to Solomon's standards in just the amount of time it takes to fall in a fishpond. This is an enchanting tale that will tickle your funny bone and tug on your heartstrings all in the same breath.

www.summersdale.com